ANTI

FULFILLING

GOD'S

DREAM

AUTHORS: Mario Arguedas; José & Silvia Barrios; Ramon & Mariela Camacho; Adelita Garza; William & Delmith Hunter; Heber & Betty Paredes; Agustín & Griselda Pérez; Frank & Dora Soto; Aldo & Liliana Suarez; Iván & Marta Villalta; Janice Larson.

ISBN: 9798396480421

Imprint: Independently published

Other books by this author:

Something Beautiful – English; El Hizo Algo Bello - Español

There was an Indian – English; Había un-Indio - Español

Miracles in Madrid – English; Milagros en Madrid - Español

Cumpliendo El Sueño de Dios – Español

IN APPRECIATION

I thank all those who encouraged me to compile this book. It has been a great honor and privilege.

First and foremost, I thank my Lord and Savior, Jesus Christ, for the missionary call He gave to my husband Richard and me to the Spanish-speaking world. It changed our trajectory and gave us an everlasting love for the Hispanic people. "Thank you, Lord!"

I want to express my gratitude to the Assemblies of God Missions Department for the privilege of serving for over thirty years with World Mission and for more than twenty-five years with US Home Missions, assigned to work with Hispanics in Southern California. We were commissioned by the Minnesota District, and we thank former Superintendent Clarence St. John and current Superintendent Mark Dean for their continuing support over the years.

I thank Superintendent Ray Rachels for inviting us to come and help in the Spanish harvest. Thank you, Superintendent Rich Guerra, for continuing to give us opportunities to serve in Hispanic Ministries and at the Hispanic School of Ministry. You have honored us, and we are very grateful.

I thank all the churches and individuals who support us financially as missionaries. You are the real heroes!

Thank you to my dear husband for sixty-five years of marriage. I have loved working by your side all these years! Forever we will be Dick and Jan (Ricardo y Juanita).

Thanks also to our four children, Melodee, Mark, Cindee, and Steve, their spouses, our twelve grandchildren, and six great-grandchildren. We love you all!

I thank these eighteen pastors who opened their hearts and shared their journey's victories and difficult moments. You are my heroes and have my highest respect. I hope readers will be inspired and challenged to pursue God's dream.

PROLOGUE

I enjoy hearing or reading other people's stories. For example, I love it when Superintendent Rich Guerra gets on the platform and says, "My father was a gardener, and now I am the superintendent of the Southern California Assemblies of God." His story encompasses the journey of his grandfather, Felipe Guerra, who emigrated from Mexico, converted to Christ, was freed from the yoke of alcohol, and founded a Hispanic Pentecostal church in a former dance hall. Brother Guerra says his life is grounded in the lessons he learned from his grandfather.

Today, attendance at churches in the SoCal Network reflects the region's demographic diversity. Some 60% of the attendees are ethnic minorities, and 40% of the Network's presbyters are non-white. In this context, it appears that God prepared Rich Guerra, with all his cultural heritage, to assume leadership of the SoCal Network at a critical moment like the present.

This anthology contains ten chapters written by eighteen Hispanic pastors and church planters in the SoCal Network of the Assemblies of God. Driven by different reasons or circumstances and with a suitcase full of dreams, they arrived in the United States from lands as diverse as Argentina, Costa Rica, Nicaragua, Guatemala, and Mexico. Others were born into the Hispanic culture here in the United States with dreams as well.

Some of them were born into Christian homes and experienced their conversion as children. Others, like the Apostle Paul, underwent a radical change as adults.

Dive into the pages of this book and discover the story of their conversion, their call to ministry, and the fantastic adventure of planting their church. As you read, you will find yourself laughing, crying, and praising God for His divine guidance, evident every step of the way.

I am privileged to know each author; we have shared many experiences. They are all true champions and heroes. Each of their stories has been written to glorify God.

Often, without even being aware, we can look back and recognize how God worked in our circumstances to bring about His perfect will.

The purposes behind the compilation of this book are as follows:

1. The fundamental purpose is that our Lord Jesus Christ receive all the honor and glory. We desire that in reading this collection of stories, the readers will profoundly understand that God has for each of them dreams, plans, and a call to service and that He is faithful to act in any way to fulfill His purpose.

2. Record and document the beginning and development of these Spanish-speaking churches in the Assemblies of God SoCal Network

3. These stories are published to assist the younger generation in learning the valuable history of their church and its beginnings. Psalm 78:5 - 7 (NIV): *"...who commanded our ancestors to teach their children, 6 so that the next generation would know them, even the children yet to be born, and they in turn would tell their children. Then they would put their trust in God and would not forget his works but would keep his commandments."*

4. Ultimately, these stories will evoke precious memories in those who lived them.

I asked God to give me the stories that would influence and encourage others, and I truly believe He has done so. I am honored to facilitate the publication of these inspiring narratives.

Authors in this Anthology.

ARGUEDAS, Mario (South Gate)

BARRIOS, José & Silvia (Bellflower)

CAMACHO, Ramon & Mariela (Huntington Park)

GARZA, Adelita (Santa Paula)

HUNTER, William & Delmith (Winterhaven)

PAREDES, Heber & Betty (Irvine)

PEREZ, Agustín & Griselda (Fresno & Madera)

SOTO, Frank & Dora (San Diego)

SUAREZ, Aldo & Liliana (Victorville)

VILLALTA, Iván & Marta (Duarte)

TABLE OF CONTENTS

1. FROM JAIL TO THE PULPIT

Pastors Frank & Dora Soto

Asambleas de Dios, El Cajon, CA

The Midnight Miracle

He was under a lot of pressure. It seems like he had lost hope and was thinking of hurting himself. However, before he did it, he opened the window curtain, expecting that someone would come and whisper, "Don't do it, don't do it!". But a voice whispered in his mind, "Do it, do it!" Before I unveil the events that followed, I want to tell you the story of our families to better understand the context.

Frank talks about his childhood

My great-grandparents on my mother's side were from Mexico. They were people with some money, but during the time of the

11

revolution, they were afraid of having everything taken from them, so they decided to flee to the state of Illinois. My mother was born there in 1921, and my father was born in Calexico, CA, so they were both U.S. citizens. My mother could read English and speak Spanish, but she could not read Spanish. My parents were not believers.

I was born on November 22, 1952. There were seven children in my family: four boys and three girls: Rigoberto, Arthur, Frank, Richard, Esther, Martha, and Liz. During our childhood, we were forced to attend the Adventist church because my paternal grandmother was an Adventist. My father did not attend church with us, but he would send us. However, I must admit that we did not learn much at that time. My younger brother and I attended services and Sunday school, even though they were held on Saturdays, but we hardly ever went inside. Instead, we would stay outside playing, and our parents assumed we were participating in the classes. My father was very strict, with a drinking problem, and used to punish us severely, leaving marks on our bodies.

We left walking but sometimes came back on bikes

I remember my childhood as normal, but now looking back, I see it differently. My father had a good job with the District Irrigation Department in Calexico, CA. We went to school, although sometimes I didn't go, but my mother didn't know it. Being four brothers, we became best friends and got involved in a lot of mischief. Sometimes we would go to El Centro, a town about thirteen or fourteen miles away, where my brother Rigoberto lived. We would walk there, but we would return on bicycles. Please don't ask me how we got the bicycles. At that time, we were seven, eight, and nine years old.

Growing up, my two older brothers chose the wrong paths. They got involved with drugs and heroin. When I was young, I wanted to use heroin, but my older brother told his friends not to give it to me. I was aware that no one would provide it to me because of the reputation of my older brother, Rigoberto. I said to my brother, "I want to try heroin." He replied, "Okay, but I will be the one to give it to you." That's how I started using this drug. I was seventeen years old, and I was already using other substances, such as barbiturates (tranquilizers) and hashish marijuana. However, thank God, I didn't use it for long.

What I enjoyed the most was heroin. My younger brother, Richard, was at death's door because he consumed such a large quantity of Barbiturates (depressants), which we called "Pingas," and did not wake up for two days. We thought he would not live, but he finally woke up. After that incident, the authorities decided to send him "up north." Since we lived in Southern California, we always referred to it as "up north," which meant he was sent to the California Youth Authority. Although he was only ten or eleven years old, my little brother was sent there for a year. The reason he was sent there, despite his young age, was because all of us, his siblings, were on probation. The judge had good intentions because he didn't want him to turn out like us, but it didn't help him at all.

Drugs for dessert

I learned that what happened in prison also happens in these institutions where there are young children. All kinds of things happen there. I was in there for using drugs and assaulting a police officer. But even there, I found an easy way to get drugs to use myself. The patients would receive prescription drugs for their illnesses, so I would trade my dessert for their drugs. There were other ways to get drugs as well, but this was the easiest for me.

Because of my two attempts to escape from the institution, I was put in a "strong room" where I was separated from the others and treated differently. I was considered a risk and was not allowed to leave for recess with the others. They locked me in a cage and left me there. It wasn't that they were bad people, but that I was an escape risk. However, during the night, two employees were in charge of the place. One of them came over, opened the door to the bunk beds where we slept, and said, "Frank," then he took me outside, offered me a cigarette, and said, "You are not like the

13

others; you are different." Taking advantage of the fact that it was nighttime, I was able to exercise outdoors. They were risking their own job by giving me this opportunity. During the day, they took me out in handcuffs. Later, I was sent "up north" to another prison. In total, I was sent "up north" three times.

Escaping from Drugs

My older brother, Rigoberto, injected heroin and had "tracks" on his arms. He was sent to San Diego to participate in a methadone program. At that time, I was not locked up and decided to call him because he had the shots, and I needed a "fix." (a dose). But thank God, at the last minute, I was unable to go! While he was waiting for me to arrive, there was a knock on his door, and my brother, who normally would not open the door without knowing who was there, opened it thinking it was me. However, they were DEA NARCO agents. They brought with them a dog that went straight for his neck. The agents said, "Don't move!" And, of course, he did not move.

Rigoberto was sent to the San Diego County jail, and although he was sick and very thin due to his heroin addiction, he got angry and started fighting with someone. My brother was going to hit him again, but instead, his fist hit the cement floor, and he broke his hand and had to be taken to the hospital with his hands and feet handcuffed, and **THIS IS WHERE THE MIRACLE HAPPENS**. A pastor whose last name was Flores from San Diego arrived and saw him handcuffed. He approached him and said, "I know who can free you from these chains!" Rigoberto heard those words but thought, "This is not possible." Of course, the pastor was talking about another kind of chain. Pastor Flores visited my brother in the hospital and gained his trust. Then, my brother was sent to the city of El Centro, in the Imperial Valley, to a center similar to Teen Challenge called "Lifeline for Youth."

When Rigoberto arrived at this institution, he found an environment centered on Bible reading and prayer. In a moment of anger, he went so far as to put a knife to the director's throat, but thank God, he did not hurt him. In spite of this, Rigoberto accepted the Lord but continued to use methadone to avoid withdrawal symptoms. One night, after a service, he turned out the lights in his room and made a request to the Lord, "If you can free me from this addiction, I will serve you." At the end of his prayer, he realized that he no longer felt the need to use drugs. That's how God delivered him from heroin. On a subsequent day, I went to give him drugs, but he told me he no longer wanted them and began to talk to me about God. All this happened in January 1973.

The whole family received Jesus as Savior because of the testimony of Rigoberto.

Rigoberto's testimony, after accepting Christ, had a significant impact on the entire Imperial Valley community. His transformation was evident to all, and to us, his family, it was apparent that something great had happened in his life. I was twenty years old at the time, and Rigoberto was twenty-four. In addition, my brother Arturo had also accepted Christ in December 1972 while in the county jail, simply through reading the Bible. We truly thank God for the power and transforming influence of the Bible!

It was in February 1973 when I had my encounter with the Lord, and from that moment, everything changed. My brother Rigoberto and I decided to fast for ten days for our younger brother, Richard, who was in a State Rehabilitation Center in Los Angeles, and they would not let him leave because he had more time to serve. So, we prayed, fasted, and soon they let him leave, and he came home and also accepted the Lord as his Savior. In a span of only four months, our whole family experienced marvelous salvation in Christ.

In my home, English was predominant, but my Spanish was a mixture of "Spanglish." When I knelt in prayer to accept the Lord as my Savior, I used what we called 'street words'. However, I experienced the powerful presence of the Lord, and my words began to flow, and I was filled at that very moment with the Holy Spirit.

Dora tells her story

"My story is simple, but beautiful. My parents and grandparents are from Michoacán, Mexico. I was born on January 16, 1956. My paternal grandmother had an eight-month-old baby who suffered from a disease unknown at the time. However, we know now that it was leprosy. Pieces of flesh would fall off her little body, and the doctor said there was no cure for this disease. At the time, she was expected to pass away due to her health condition, and she had even stopped crying.

An Instant Miracle

One day a neighbor came and told my grandmother, "I know someone who can heal her. I will take you to someone who prays to God, and people get healed." But in those years, Christians were being persecuted, and the neighbor said, "Don't tell anyone I took you there!" My grandmother was full of fear, but they decided to take the baby to that person, who turned out to be a pastor. He prayed fervently for the baby and told my grandmother that she should accept Christ. However, she, being Catholic, did not understand those words very well.

The pastor placed his hand on the baby and continued praying. Realizing that the baby was no longer crying, my grandmother thought she was dead or sleeping. However, when they got home, my grandmother noticed that the baby was breathing and put her to bed, where she slept the whole night through. In the morning, my grandmother removed the baby's blankets, and her skin was like that of a newborn. It was an instant miracle! The Lord had healed the baby while the pastor prayed for her. Although my grandmother did not follow the Lord closely, she did feel Christ in her heart.

My grandparents moved to San Luis, Sonora, Mexico. My grandmother did not know how to read but listened to Christian programs on the radio. My brother and I suffered from a skin infection similar to ingrown pimples. When I was five years old, my grandmother called us to listen to Pastor Roberto Fiero on the radio because he was saying, "Put your hand on the radio, the Lord will heal you." Those pimples caused me so much pain, but I had a lot of faith. My brother and I placed our hands on the radio, and the Lord healed us.

We continued living in San Luis, Sonora, Mexico, except for my dad, who lived in the United States. Then, he decided to buy a house in Mexicali, Baja California, in order to be closer to his family. Not too much later, we all moved to Mexicali. It was there that we heard loudspeakers making announcements about a church, and that is how my grandmother, my brother, and I began to attend. I felt that the Lord had something special for me in that place. My mother, who was Catholic, did not attend with us and showed no interest in anything related to God.

The Lord saved me and baptized me in the Holy Spirit

When I was nine years old, I experienced a significant encounter with the Lord. I remember that moment vividly. Although we regularly attended an independent church, one night, our pastor was invited to preach at a youth service at an Assemblies of God church. We decided to accompany him, and it was there that I made the decision to accept Christ as my Savior. As an innocent nine-year-old child, I opened my heart to Him.

Three days after my conversion to Christ, I experienced a strong desire to attend the women's prayer group that was held at nine o'clock in the morning. I begged my mother to let me go to pray, but she would not let me miss school. However, the meeting was being held in a house that was very close to the school, so I decided to attend the prayer without my mother's permission. When my knees touched the floor at that prayer meeting, the Holy Spirit descended upon me, and I began to speak in tongues. I started at ten o'clock in the morning, and by three o'clock in the afternoon, I still could not stop speaking in tongues. It was a powerful experience in which the Lord baptized me in the Holy Spirit.

My mom, worried that I had not returned home from school, came looking for me. When she found me, she tried to talk to me, and I wanted to respond, but I could only speak in tongues. This impressed her because when she attended church, she thought people who spoke in tongues were crazy. However, upon hearing her daughter speak in tongues without receiving instructions from anyone, she was deeply impacted and accepted the Lord through this experience.

Throughout my youth, I faced some small temptations, but I never abandoned my commitment to the Lord or to the church. From the age of twelve, I clearly felt God's call to serve Him. I began to get involved in the ministry of the church by helping young children in Sunday School. My walk with the Lord was evident through my service and dedication to his work.

Frank: I wanted to serve the Lord

I can't pinpoint the exact moment I received a specific call to serve God, but I felt a strong desire to do something for the Lord. The day after I accepted Christ, my brothers and I were out preaching on the streets. We would stop the cars and share about Christ, maybe a little aggressively. We would walk the streets on our way to church, preaching to everyone we met, and the people would listen to us.

To learn more about God and to serve Him better, Rigoberto, Richard, and I decided to live at the Lifeline Institute for two or three years. It was during this time that I saw Dora for the first time. She claims to have seen me before and remembers liking my long hair very much.

I helped out at the church, El Sendero de la Cruz, where Sister Fox was the pastor. There I had the responsibility of supervising the youth. However, I felt the need to continue learning, and I enrolled in the Bethany Bible Institute in Tijuana, Mexico. The Spanish language was quite difficult for me, I did not know how to write correctly in that language, but thank God, He helped me! Studying the Bible was the easiest for me because I had read it before. The second year was when Dora came as a student.

Dora: *"How will I get to the Institute?"*

Everyone in my family was now a believer, although my father never fully surrendered to the Lord. He had other families on the side but always provided the essentials for us. However, from a very young age, we began to work to cover our expenses and help our mother. When I felt the call to study the Bible, I decided to enroll in LABI, the Latin American Bible Institute in La Puente, California. I was excited and had prepared all the documents to enroll. I had my registration ready when my father said, "You can go, but don't expect a dime from me. I can't help you. If you decide to go, you will have to pay the entire cost of school on your own because I won't be able to help you."

I worked all summer, but I was not able to raise the full amount of money I needed to cover all the expenses for the school year. At that time, Pastor Fox suggested to me, "Why don't you consider going to Bethany Bible Institute in Tijuana. It's cheaper, it's closer, and you speak Spanish very well. It would even be easier for you to go there". I didn't know Frank was there. I explained to Pastor Fox that I didn't know where Bethany was located and that classes were about to start. So, she talked to the director of the Bible Institute, and they gave me the opportunity to enter without the formal application and gave me the date when I should be there. However, I still had the challenge of how to get to the Bible Institute, as I did not know its location. It was then that Sister Fox reassured me by saying, "Don't you worry, Frank is there." At the mention of Frank's name, I remembered that I knew him, even though I had not seen him for a long time. I obtained Frank's phone number through his uncle, but I was somewhat embarrassed to call him and ask for help in getting to Bethany Bible Institute. Anyway, I called, and although Frank did not have a car, his brother Rigoberto drove us to Tijuana. This is the way Frank and I arrived at the Institute together.

Suddenly, something extraordinary happened; we started to fall in love with each other. One day, while a group of us were working together in the kitchen, we started talking about whom we each liked. I didn't want to reveal that I liked Frank, but I finally confided in someone and told him whom I had a crush on, but I asked him not to mention it to anyone. Not five minutes passed when one of the young people went to find Frank in the chapel and started talking to him.

We were married on April 15, 1978

Frank: I was in the chapel, spending my time praying to the Lord, looking for a sign to tell me if Dora had feelings for me. I asked the Lord in my prayers, "If Dora loves me, please send me a sign; let someone come and tell me if she loves me." As soon as I finished my prayer, a brother came up to me and said excitedly, "Frank, Frank. I just found out that Dora loves you". That was a clear sign from God to me. From the chapel, I could see Dora, and I approached her to express my feelings, "I love you in the Lord. Will you marry me?" Although Dora did not give an affirmative answer at the time, we both knew that it was our destiny to marry. I had asked the Lord for a woman who loved God above all else, and in Dora, I found that quality.

All this happened in November, a few months after the start of classes. Dora was nineteen years old. We went to our homes for Christmas vacation, and when we returned to the Bible Institute, Dora was already wearing her engagement ring. In May, I graduated and began working at a church in Calexico. Dora returned to Bethany for her sophomore year, but unfortunately, she contracted pneumonia and was unable to complete the academic year. Finally, on April 15, 1978, we were married.

1978 - 1991 Unpaid Helpers

During this period, we were very involved in the service of the church under the guidance of Pastor Fox. We actively participated in various activities such as weddings, baptisms, and many other responsibilities. We both served as unpaid assistants. In addition, I served as chaplain at the county jail and also preached at youth services, among other ministry responsibilities. Our lives were very busy from 1978 to 1991. In addition, we started a church in

Holtville, California. I had ministerial credentials with the Southern Pacific District.

We came very close to becoming pastors of a church in Azusa, California. We left our jobs and our home in hopes of assuming that role, but in the end, the pastor in charge decided not to leave his position. We found ourselves in a difficult situation since we no longer had a home. Our two children and Dora and I were forced to live in a room at Sister Fox's church. It was a very challenging time for us. One night, Dora had a dream, and in the morning, she excitedly told me about it. In her dream, she saw me preaching in a church where there were people of different races and nationalities. At the time, I joked that maybe her dream was because she had eaten too many beans. We both laughed at that quip. We continued to assist and help Sister Fox for two more years, although we had no formal titles or positions. During that time, we also started a family business that prospered, allowing us to finally move into an apartment and improve our living conditions.

It was a Confirmation

My dream, my longing all my life, was to dedicate myself to full-time ministry. One Sunday, missionary Harry Bartel attended one of our church services. He was involved in a church planting program called Decade of Harvest. Brother Bartel knew me because he had been my teacher at the Bible Institute. During his visit, missionary Bartel informed us that Pastor Ron Casen of Centro Assembly in El Cajon had a passion for reaching the Hispanic community and was looking for someone to start a ministry in that area. He asked if we would be interested in speaking with Pastor Casen about this opportunity. Without hesitation, we responded in the affirmative. We made an appointment to travel to the city of El Cajon with Brother Bartel.

In December 1990, we arrived at Brother Casen's church. We went directly to the office and introduced ourselves to him, he received us kindly and invited us to go to the sanctuary. The sanctuary had two doors on each side and two doors in the center.

When those doors opened, something amazing happened. Dora instantly remembered vividly what she had dreamed. Everything she was seeing at that moment, the carpet, the chairs, the pulpit, and the crescent-shaped platform, were exactly the same as what she had experienced in her dream. Dora excitedly exclaimed, "Frank, this is the church I saw in my dream." This was an unmistakable confirmation that we were in the place where God was leading us and wanted us.

On January 6, 1991, we planted the El Cajon, Asambleas de Dios (Assemblies of God church)

We left behind our business, salary, and apartment and came with nothing, accompanied by our children and confident in our faith in God. By then, Arthur was three, Frankie was eight, and Giselle was eleven. As we started the church, we took on multiple roles. We were the drivers, the cleaners and were willing to do any task necessary. One Sunday after the service, everyone had left except for a couple whose wife was about seven or eight months pregnant, another lady, and our own family. Our children were waiting for us.

Suddenly, the lady came running up and informed us in alarm, "Pastor, pastor, there's someone outside in a car driving around in circles, and I'm scared." I immediately left to observe the situation. It was an Anglo man, tall and thin, who was driving around in circles at the entrance of the church. At that moment, the man stared at me, pointed his finger at me, and said in English, "I have been following you since the Imperial Valley. I hate you, and I am going to destroy you." I looked around and saw the pregnant woman as her husband rushed over with a chair to protect me. Although I was facing that Anglo man, I recognized that the one challenging me was the enemy, the devil. So I replied, "I know who you are too." I considered laying my hands on him and rebuking the enemy, but seeing the pregnant woman, I was worried that she might go into labor at that very moment because of the tense situation.

Therefore, I decided to reassure the man and told him that was fine, which caused him to finally back off. He never reappeared after that incident.

"Take them away; they are yours."

The church was experiencing rapid and remarkable growth, so much so that I received a plaque of recognition from the city of El Cajon. Around the area of the church, there were three gangs: the LOCOS, the DUQUES, and the ORFANOS, who fought a lot with each other. However, we decided to get involved with them and organized a big evangelistic crusade in the parking lot of the church, where about thirty people accepted Christ as their Savior. It was a significant event where we even received support from the police to control traffic, which was a great blessing.

That night, a person came who was not from our church but was a minister and was already working with gangs. At the end of the event, those who had accepted Christ went to the sanctuary to receive orientation about their new Christian life. As I entered the sanctuary, I saw that this person who was not from our church was already talking to them. I didn't want to cause any harm to the new converts, so I told the minister, "Take them away, they are yours." And he took almost all of them to his church. He had experience with this type of population and was actively working with them. The most important thing to me was that these people had found God, and I was not going to allow disputes or arguments to arise in front of them.

Satan's attacks

God was doing wonders in our church. Children were being baptized in the Holy Spirit, and we witnessed many miracles in our midst. However, after such a beautiful time of revival, we noticed that problems arose in the church, and I firmly believe it was an attempt by the enemy; the devil, to destroy us. We found ourselves facing attacks from people within the church who sought to take over the leadership. They had a lot of influence, and unfortunately, before they left our church, they caused a lot of damage to the congregation. It was painful to realize that even within the church, there were such cruel people. These situations affected me deeply, especially because my children were hurt in the process. My eight-year-old son, Frankie, looked up to his Royal Rangers commander but heard this leader speak ill of me to someone else, which caused him great pain. My daughter also heard a sister speak ill of us, and this caused her to cry deeply. In addition to being pastors, we are parents first and foremost, and we are pained by the negative effect that situations like this have on our children. They hurt our children very much.

El Cajon A/D moves to a new location

The reason we decided to leave the American church in El Cajon was because Pastor Casen left his pastoral position. In his place came Pastor Al Roundtree, who had a different vision from ours. He wanted to unite the two churches, the American and the Hispanic, under one entity, and we did not agree with that structure. We wanted to maintain our identity and autonomy as a Hispanic church. Of course, there are always challenges when two churches share a physical space. But we are very appreciative of Brother Al Roundtree and his wife. We appreciate their kind treatment of us, and we value their support. After twelve years, we made the decision to leave the American church facilities in April 2003.

We moved to the Christian Mall

In April 2003, our church found a new location at 389 N. Magnolia Ave, El Cajon, CA. Originally, the location had been a movie theater complex but was now renting spaces to various churches. People commented that this former movie theater mall had now become a church mall or Christian mall. It was there that we experienced the greatest growth and development as a congregation.

The years we spent there were years of many blessings and spiritual rest. We remained there for a period of ten years. In August 2013, we were forced to move due to the sale of the property.

We moved to the Masonic Lodge

On August 18, 2013, we moved to the current location where we are renting, the Masonic Lodge located at 695 Ballantyne St., El Cajon. Here we hold our services on Sundays and a few other days of the month. A year later, on August 19, 2014, we decided to rent a second location to establish a Ministry Center in El Cajon. In this center, we have spaces designated for smaller meetings during the week, such as men's, women's, and children's groups. We use the Ministry Center practically every day for different activities, and we have the church office in our house.

Our own building

You ask me, how is the experience of not having your own building? The main difference is that we don't have the freedom to make changes or place objects as we would like. At the Ministry Center, however, it is almost like having our own building. Here we can organize the space according to our needs and leave everything ready for our activities. At the Masonic Lodge, where we conduct our services, we must set up and take down the instruments and chairs at each service. This involves additional work and requires time and effort. In contrast, at the Ministry Center, we can keep everything ready and prepared. In San Diego or El Cajon, it is really difficult and expensive to find a church building to purchase. Real estate prices are high, which makes it difficult to acquire a space of one's own. That is why many churches continue to rent.

Lack of maturity

If I could start in ministry again with the knowledge I have now, I would do things very differently. The priority for me would be to make sure I protect and care for my wife and children so that they are not mistreated.

The other aspect would be to work with greater maturity. My lack of maturity at that time affected some areas of my life. As we met at Central Assembly in El Cajon, we experienced the Lord's work in our church. The Lord used me through spiritual gifts, and when I spoke under the anointing of God, I experienced an inexplicable confidence. However, I began to notice that some of the brethren saw me as a miracle worker. They would say, "There goes my pastor," or "That's my pastor." I did not want to be the center of attention since it was the Lord who worked the miracles, and the glory should go to Christ. But in an act of immaturity, I prayed an unwise prayer. I told the Lord, "I don't want this," and as a result, some of the spiritual gifts in my life stopped. I admit it was a lack of maturity on my part at the time.

Nine months of treatment

We have gone through several diseases. In my case, I was diagnosed with psoriasis of the liver. The doctor told me I had psoriasis and prescribed nine months of treatment. During that time, I could barely walk and took pills three times a day. Without the treatment, the next stage would be cancer # 4. Although my liver is damaged, there is still a part of it that is working properly, and this is what gives me life. I feel fine, although I still have to go to the doctor from time to time. Before, I spent most of my time in bed, except on Sundays when I left to preach. Now I am fine, and I don't even need to take pills.

The Midnight Miracle Story continues

We are sharing this story to let people know about the power of the Lord in our lives. Our son was facing great pressure and had lost all hope, even considering taking his own life. In a desperate moment, he opened the window curtain expecting someone to come up to him and say, "Don't do it! Don't do it!". However, a voice in his mind told him otherwise, "Do it, do it!". Fortunately, a member of our family found him in time and called an ambulance. We quickly rushed to the hospital and found him in critical condition, with almost no vital signs. He had been seventeen minutes without oxygen. He remained intubated and motionless. But my wife, Dora, had an unwavering faith and constantly reminded God of the promise He had made to her that our son would serve the Lord.

Dora continues to tell us the story. At that time, many friends and family members came to the hospital to pray for our son. Among them were my brother and sister-in-law. Before leaving, my sister-in-law shared an idea she had heard from a minister about the "midnight miracle." According to her, she had heard that at midnight, the Lord performed amazing miracles. It was then that she suggested, "Let us pray for the "midnight miracle." With great faith and hope, we began to pray, asking the Lord to perform a miracle and raise our son. My sister-in-law concluded her prayer by saying, "We ask you for the "midnight miracle," Lord." Then, we said our goodbyes, and she left, leaving our requests in the Lord's hands.

It was time for the nurses' shift change, and unfortunately, we could not be in the room with our son. Our daughter-in-law wanted to check on her husband, so she decided to go into the room. Upon entering, she thought she saw him move and screamed for joy. However, in the midst of the confusion, we feared that she was crying because she thought he was already dead. She came running out of the room, screaming, and told us that she had noticed movement in our son. We all rushed into the room, and at that moment, the nurse said, "Talk to him because he has reacted with his eyes. Keep talking to him, he seems to be listening to you." I spoke to him, and he started to look at me. In that instant, hope was reborn, at least we knew he was still alive.

He was now answering our questions. Although he could not speak because of the tube in his throat, he would nod his head and touched our hands to communicate. He knew where he was and who he was. We began to thank the Lord for his evident recovery. However, at that moment, the enemy, the devil, tried to sow doubts in my thoughts. I wondered, "How is his mind? He went seventeen minutes without oxygen, could there be any brain damage?". I was having a battle in my thoughts. I began to pray and asked the Lord that everything would be perfect. But doubts kept nagging me, "How will his mind be after so many minutes without oxygen?"

The next day, we met with a group of doctors. They all looked at us in amazement, and one of them, a woman, laughed, patted me on the shoulder, and said, "I don't know, I don't know! Someone up there is watching because this doesn't happen every day!" I replied, "I know!". The doctors recognized that it was an act of God. They asked us to sit down and said, "When your son was admitted to the ER, we ran tests, and no brain activity was detected. Everything in the readings was dark and worrisome. However, this morning when we re-ran the tests, everything lit up as if nothing had happened." I instantly exclaimed, "Thank God!". I was certain that everything was going to be fine. Now, many years later, our son has a good job, and everything is fine. "I want people to know what the Lord did!"

We are happy serving the Lord

We are very happy serving the Lord! Oh yes, very, very, very happy! We wouldn't trade these years for anything. We have been with this church for thirty-one years now.

In spite of the time that has passed, the church we have today is like the abundant harvest of all that we have sown throughout these years. It is a congregation that loves us, cares for us, works hard, and is very faithful. I have known some churches that, during the pandemic, lost members and experienced financial difficulties, but in our case, we have seen an increase in our finances, and the people are still here, showing their unconditional love. Sometimes, I say to the Lord, "This is a gift from you, not because we deserve it, but because of your work in our midst." When I look at the church, I can feel their love and protection. They care about us. I often tell the brethren, "We won't always be here, but while we are here, I want you to learn to value your pastors. When the time comes for another pastor to assume leadership, I want you to love and support him as you have loved and supported us."

Sometimes it seems as if we are about to wake up from a dream because the church has undergone a total transformation; it is no longer the same church we had at the beginning. Dora and I have also changed, we have grown in our faith and in our service to the

Lord. The brethren value us, and we love each one of them as if they were our own children. They take care of us and protect us with so much love that sometimes, they do not allow us to do anything. Even when we want to get involved in some tasks, they tell us, "No, pastor, do not deprive us of the blessing of helping you."

The Lord has shown us that in our church, there are highly qualified people, and therefore, they should use their abilities for the edification of the body of Christ. We are now assigning them more responsibilities, and they are ready for it.

Our vision is that the congregation will be strengthened in the Lord and prepared to establish new churches.

2. WE HAVE TRULY BEEN HAPPY!

Pastors William & Delmith Hunter

Vida Abundante & Abundant Life, Winterhaven, CA

"The American Dream"

It was almost two o'clock in the afternoon, sometime in January 1993. I was in the supply and janitorial room of the First Assembly of God Church in Wilmington, California, where I was working as a janitor. This was the first job God had given me when I came to the United States from Guatemala, along with my wife and two-and-a-half-year-old daughter.

We decided to leave behind what we had in search of a better future. We left our house, which we had recently bought; I left my studies at the university and my job with an American company, and of course, we left our families behind. Initially, we only came to visit, but once here, I suggested to my wife that we stay, and she agreed, although she was not completely convinced. We were full of dreams and illusions; we longed for a better life, the "American dream," which meant working hard and earning money.

I said, "Yes, Lord!"

The presence of the Lord was very strong at that moment, practically irresistible. It was then that I fell on my knees before Him and said, "Yes, Lord, I accept your call to serve you in whatever you desire, wherever, whenever. I surrender myself completely to you. I now understand that what my soul truly longs for is to serve you, not to pursue the "American Dream." I renounce the simple desire to accumulate wealth." Then I made a covenant with the Lord, saying, "From this day forward, I will serve you with all my heart in every way I can, and you will take care of me and my family, providing everything we need." It was sad to realize, that up to that point, I seemed to desire material things more than serving God, and that was preventing me from obeying His call to serve Him.

I may be interested

The truth is that it never crossed my mind to be a pastor, minister, evangelist, or anything like that. My plan was to go out into the streets to evangelize, and for those who believed in the gospel, to take them to church to be discipled.

Since I had made the decision to serve the Lord, a few days later, I told the youth pastor, Mike Hinojosa, that I wanted to study the Word of God more. I had seen some Berean School of the Bible folders in his office. He gave me the necessary information about this school and encouraged me to study. To my surprise, a few days later, he called me into his office and told me that he had received a call from the Southern California District (Network) inviting him to pastor a small church in the desert. He stated that he did not believe it was God's will for him but mentioned that he knew someone working in his church who was interested in serving the Lord. Of course, it was me. He told them I might be interested in going to pastor that church. I was twenty-nine years old at the time. He gave me a phone number and asked me to talk to Fred Cottriel, who would explain everything to me.

A pastor? Me a pastor of a church? As I said before, it was not what I had been thinking, but a few days earlier, I had completely surrendered to the Lord and promised to serve Him wherever, whenever and however He wanted me to. How could I back out now and say no to Jesus? It seemed that the Lord had been working on a plan and was just waiting for me to surrender myself completely to Him to put that plan into action.

William: I gave my heart to the Lord at eighteen years of age

Our story began in 1983 when I believed in Jesus as my Savior and made Him the Lord of my life. After that, I often heard the Lord calling me to serve Him through the messages and teachings in the church I attended. I tried to do this mainly with the youth because I had just turned eighteen. I continued to do this for about seven years until we moved to the United States.

When we arrived in the United States, we joined a Hispanic group that met in the church where I worked, and I began to help Brother Tijerina, who was in charge of the group. I always knew that I should serve the Lord and understood that it was the responsibility of every believer. Although I felt that the Lord wanted more from me, I must emphasize that I had never contemplated being a pastor.

Interestingly, I remember on one occasion, during a service at the church we were attending in Guatemala, the assistant pastor shared a word from the Lord. However, before doing so, he asked if young Bill (that's what everyone called me) was present in that meeting, to which someone answered no. He then claimed to have received a word from the Lord that I would become a pastor. When this message was told to me, I listened with interest, but I honestly

33

did not believe it could come true. My wife also had some dreams in which she saw me preaching to groups of people. Although I found those dreams interesting, I never gave them much thought at the time.

Delmith accepted Jesus as her Savior at the age of eight

My wife, Delmith, accepted Jesus at the age of eight during a children's campaign. Her father had abandoned the family a year earlier. As a result of that difficult situation, her mother had given her life to the Lord. My wife relates that when she was seventeen, a sister from church approached her and told her that the Lord had a ministry for her. Delmith thought it would be in singing (as she loved to sing), or perhaps traveling to different places, but she certainly never imagined it would be the ministry of pastoring a church.

A small church in the desert needs a Pastor

After my conversation with Pastor Mike, I called Fred Cottriel, who informed me about a small church in a desert town called Winterhaven that needed a pastor. However, he did not give me many details about the town, or the church, which left many questions in my mind at the end of the conversation. I didn't know if the church had a congregation, however small, or if it was closed. I also wondered if I would have to preach in English, Spanish, or bilingual. I didn't know what type of building it was, as well as details about the size of the population, community, and so forth. I recall Fred mentioning that there was a growing Hispanic population that needed to be reached, as well as the presence of the indigenous community in the area. At the end of our conversation, Fred expressed interest in meeting me in person and mentioned that I would also have to speak with George Wood, the assistant superintendent. We set up a date and time for me to visit the district (Network)offices and conduct these meetings.

That day I had the opportunity to meet Brother Cottriel personally. After greeting each other, he took me directly to George

34

Wood's office. There, Brother Wood asked me some general questions, such as how long I had been a believer, whether I had received the Baptism in the Holy Spirit, and especially, why I believed I was the right candidate to pastor the church in Winterhaven. In response, I told him about the experience I had recently and what had happened since then. I explained that I did not consider myself qualified to pastor that church, but that I was willing to do whatever Jesus asked me to do. If He called me to that town, then I would obey Him without reservation.

I was willing to go anywhere

As I left George Wood's office, Brother Cottriel went in to talk with him. When he came out, he told me everything looked fine. My interview with Brother Wood took about five minutes. We then arranged with Brother Cottriel to make a trip to the church in Winterhaven on February 25, my wife Delmith's birthday. We would meet at the District (Network) offices and go in his car. It would be an all-day trip, as Winterhaven was about four hours away from Irvine.

Since we had only recently arrived in the United States and were unfamiliar with many places (up to that point, we only knew Los Angeles County and some of its cities). When I learned that the church was in the desert, I imagined a desert landscape like the ones in the old Western movies, with very little vegetation, scarcity of water, mountains of stone, intense heat, and a wind blowing and rolling dry bushes. In addition, I thought that the houses in the town would be simple like shacks with clay walls and thatched roofs. At that moment, I realized that God seemed to be serious about my commitment to give up comfort, and I was willing to follow His call no matter where He called me, for I had promised Him.

Delmith was visiting her family in Guatemala

Two and a half years had passed without Delmith being able to reunite with her family, whom she was eager to see. This was her first return to Guatemala since we moved to the United States in July 1990. I had not been able to accompany her due to financial constraints. In fact, I decided to work during my vacation so that she could travel with our two children.

So, I had not mentioned anything to Delmith about the possibility of pastoring in Winterhaven since she was in Guatemala.

Would she venture to go to such a desolate and destitute place, would she share my determination to serve the Lord in any circumstance, would she be willing to give up everything along with me, would she agree to take our children, and many more questions? Until now, I had not revealed to her anything about my total surrender or my decision to serve God fully. I had not informed her about my conversation with Pastor Mike or Fred Cottriel. In fact, I had mentioned nothing.

We lived in a modest, one-bedroom apartment next to the church where I worked. When my family left for Guatemala, I imagined that I would finally have time to rest a little more and perhaps watch a movie in the evenings. It was challenging living with two small children in such a small place. At first, that's what I did when I came home from work: I would turn on the TV for a while and then start drawing until late at night. In Guatemala, I had begun my studies in architecture, and my wife's uncle generously gave me the opportunity to create illustrations for the rubber company he worked for, which allowed me to earn a little extra money.

However, that routine did not last long because the Lord and His Holy Spirit began to work in my life in an extraordinary way. The Lord drew near to me, urging me to draw closer to Him. I increased my Bible reading and prayer time, and as the days went by, I felt closer and closer to God until I reached that moment of surrender in the supply room.

I wanted to be entirely sure

Everything was happening so quickly. The decision to move to Winterhaven and take over the pastorate would be a total change in our lives. Although my heart recognized God's work in all this, I longed for absolute certainty. So, I did something that would confirm that it was from God. In deep prayer, I said to the Lord, "If this is truly from you, I pray that you will be the one to reveal it to my wife in Guatemala. When she returns, she will understand the call you are making to us, and I am not going to say a word about it." Although Delmith and I kept in touch through letters and sporadic phone calls (since cell phones did not exist back then and internet access was limited), I reiterate that this particular matter had not been mentioned at all.

"It is essential that you support your husband"

The day of my beloved family's return finally arrived. I went to pick them up at the airport, carrying a bouquet of flowers for my wife, I missed them so much! They left the plane, and we hugged and kissed.

On the way to our apartment, Delmith told me the following story that happened in Guatemala. She had received a call from Sister Aminta (an acquaintance of hers from Guatemala with whom she had not had any contact for years). Sister Aminta asked her daughters if they had any information about my wife, to which they replied that they had heard that she was visiting family in Guatemala. Sister Aminta told her daughters that she needed to talk to my wife because she had a word from the Lord for her. When they finally got in touch, Sister Aminta told my wife that when she prayed the night before, the Lord had told her that He would move us to a place where she would be very happy. My wife immediately asked her if it would be there in Guatemala, because where else would she be so happy? Sister Aminta told her that she did not know the place but added that it was very important that she support me. "It Is very important that you support your husband," God said.

The Lord had answered my request

As my wife shared the story with me, I felt my heart turn over in my chest, for the Lord had answered my prayer and revealed His plan for us. I immediately began to relate to her all that had transpired in her absence, as she listened in reverent silence. I remember her expressing to me a mixture of doubt and fear regarding the call to be pastors. During her childhood, she lived for a time with her aunt and uncle, who were pastors and had witnessed the sacrifice and scarcity involved in that path. Understandably, those memories had planted seeds of apprehension and questioning in her heart.

The call was for both of us

The Lord whispered deep within me and prompted me to share two points with her. First, I assured her that I would not force her to do anything. I told her that it was essential that she also accept God's call of her own free will. If she decided to accept, then together we would embark on that path, but if her answer was no, I would respect her decision, and I promised her that I would never reproach her or even bring up the subject again. Secondly, I expressed to her that if she accepted the call, I would dedicate myself to service in the church, while she would assume the role of being my partner and raising our children. I recognized at that moment, that those words did not come from my own wisdom, but were inspired by the Holy Spirit; for upon hearing them, Delmith did not feel pressured but invited by God's will. The call was for both of us, not just for me. Nor did she feel overwhelmed thinking she also had to do the work of a pastor. That gave her peace and tranquility in the depths of her heart.

The long-awaited day arrived for our trip to Winterhaven to visit the church. We met Brother Cottriel in the parking lot of the Network office. We got into his car and headed for Imperial County. It was the first time we had driven through San Diego, then up through the towering stone mountains past the city of El Cajon, finally descending into the vast desert. It was February, and although the desert reflected the image I had imagined, at least the temperature was pleasant during that month.

We continued our journey and arrived in the city of El Centro, where we had the privilege of meeting with the presbyter of the Imperial Valley section, Pastor Bill Brewer. We also met with Pastor Isaí Quiñónez, leader of the church in Calexico, who spoke Spanish and with whom we felt very comfortable. Although my father was American, I was born and raised in Guatemala, so he did not speak much English to us. For that reason, and thanks to my studies in school, I understood English quite well and could communicate, although I was still in the process of learning. My wife, on the other hand, only knew what little she had been taught at school.

A rather poor and small place

Upon arriving in Winterhaven, the picture became clearer, and my perception began to change. The place was not as I had imagined it, and I thank God for that, because the fact that I had conceived such an unfavorable image at the beginning, helped me at that moment to appreciate it in its true essence. If I had imagined a more beautiful place, I might not have found it as attractive as it turned out to be.

Winterhaven, a picturesque town surrounded by the Indigenous Reservation, sprawls over an area of just 0.2 square miles, making it possible to walk it in a matter of minutes. When we first arrived in Winterhaven, its population hovered around seven hundred people, although, over time, it has decreased significantly. According to the 2020 census, there were only one hundred and fifty-one inhabitants. Undoubtedly, it is a modest place of small dimensions. The church had a small building consisting of a main hall built with adobe in the 1930s. Over time, small outbuildings were added around the main building. The sanctuary had a maximum capacity of approximately eighty people. The church also provided a spacious mobile home for the pastors, with three bedrooms, two bathrooms, and in good condition. In addition, they had a van that could accommodate fifteen passengers.

One of Winterhaven's notable advantages is its proximity to Yuma, Arizona, a considerably more populous city. At that time, in 1993, Yuma had about sixty thousand residents, a number that has grown significantly to approximately ninety-eight thousand residents today. So, Winterhaven is not completely isolated, and that let us know that we could work hard to reach out and serve the people of Yuma as well.

Is this the place where we will be happy?

We entered the small church, which had been closed for several months. In Winterhaven, there were two Assemblies of God churches. The one we were in, was a white church, and the other, was an indigenous church. The Lord had moved these two English-speaking congregations to join together and make facilities available to reach Spanish-speaking people. At that moment, we realized God had been planning, working, and preparing to bring us to this place. God is always at work! The church had pews and red carpet, all quite old, with dust and cobwebs. Then we went to see the parsonage, and Pastor Brewer asked my wife if she liked it. My wife tells me that although she said yes, it wasn't the house that impressed her or the fact that our children would have a room for each of them, but it was the church that impressed her. Delmith especially remembers seeing a plaster figure of hands joined together as if praying, but with cobwebs around it. As we stood inside the little sanctuary, she asked the Lord if this would be the place where she would be happy.

Our visit to Winterhaven and the church lasted about an hour and a half. Then we returned to our apartment. My wife had not yet expressed her thoughts to me. I did not know if she wanted to accept the responsibility of pastoring the church in Winterhaven and if she was willing to accept the Lord's call. However, since it was her birthday, her family in Guatemala called her to give her a special greeting. As quickly as she initiated the conversation with her mother, the first thing Delmith said to her was, "We are going to Winterhaven." I understood at that moment that her answer was a resounding yes to God's call.

We opened the church on Sunday, May 16, 1993

We moved to Winterhaven on April 29, 1993, and opened the church on Sunday, May 16, 1993. In our first service, we had five children present who didn't live in Winterhaven but in the surrounding areas. Some of our first services were just my family and me. On one occasion, we asked the Lord to give us one family from Winterhaven and one from Yuma to help us start.

Of course, we knocked on doors to invite the neighbors. One day, while visiting houses in the area, we came across a little girl, about five years old, outside a house. We asked her if her parents were inside, and she informed us that her mother, aunt, and nana were there. Then the grandmother came outside to find out who we were. When we told her that we were the new pastors in the area and that we were conducting services in Spanish, she told us that her son was not there and that her daughter-in-law was sick with kidney stones and would have an operation in the next few days.

At that moment, the girl's father arrived, and after introducing ourselves, we asked him if we could pray for his wife, and he said yes. We found that she was in bed, pale and in much pain. We joined in prayer, asking the Lord to heal her, and then said our goodbyes. The following Sunday, the whole family came to church and told us that the same afternoon after we had prayed for her, the pain disappeared, and it was no longer necessary for her to undergo surgery. It was a moment of joy and gratitude where we recognized the power and goodness of God in our lives.

Another Sunday, a new family arrived, and when we greeted them, they told us they were from Yuma. They were looking for another church, but when they couldn't find one and saw ours, they decided to come in. We were happy to receive them, and we thanked God because this family was the answer to the prayer we had prayed. We already had a family from Winterhaven, and now this family from Yuma. From that moment on, they began to attend regularly. Little by little, the Lord began to bring people. Since we did not have musicians in the church and were not musicians ourselves, my wife led the singing with a tape recorder and cassette. As more people began to attend, they invited their family and friends, which contributed to the growth of the church. As time went by, the church grew, mainly with people from Yuma. We are grateful to God that, in spite of being located in a small place, our attendance has always been high in proportion to the size of the place.

Twenty-nine years and still in Winterhaven

A few weeks after we arrived in Winterhaven, I prayerfully told the Lord I would stay in Winterhaven as long as He wanted us there. I told Him that if He wanted to take us somewhere else, He should reveal it to us in a manner similar to that which He had used to bring us here. Now twenty-nine years have passed, and we are still in Winterhaven. Throughout this time, we have received invitations to pastor in other places on at least three occasions, but we have not considered it to be God's will. There was one occasion when, due to a personal crisis, I was tempted to leave the church and go elsewhere, but the Lord strengthened me, and I remained here. It is evident that He has been by our side, comforting and strengthening us. We have found that there is no better place to be than where we are in God's will, and yes, both Delmith and I have been truly happy!

Throughout these years, the Lord has allowed us to see numerous lives surrendered to Him, amazing miracles, and people restored and healed. We have had the privilege of baptizing countless people, providing discipleship, praying for the sick, witnessing the Holy Spirit poured out on them, dedicating many children, performing marriages, and participating in many funerals. Our commitment also extends to the support of missionaries, giving them support to the best of our ability. The Lord has also blessed us with the privilege of being part of the lives of people who are now pastoring other congregations. In 2001, we built a larger sanctuary with a capacity for two hundred people.

In addition, I was blessed to complete my studies at the Berean School of the Bible up to the ordination level. Eventually, we also established our own church study center, where we had fifty-six students studying, some of whom, as I mentioned, are now pastors.

During these thirty years, we have also been an active part of the Southern California Network of the Assemblies of God.

We now have two congregations

In August 2021, we received a special call from the SoCal Network of the Assemblies of God to take on the responsibility of pastoring the other church in our town. This new challenge has led us to have two congregations under our care, one in Spanish and one in English, known as Vida Abundante and Abundant Life, respectively. We remain steadfast in serving and thankful to our Savior, Jesus Christ.

A special recognition

I give special recognition to my beloved wife, Delmith, who is an integral part of the ministry and whom the Lord called along with me. She has sacrificially and selflessly stood by my side, supporting me, serving in many of the congregation's ministries, managing our home, and raising our three children. The Lord called us both, we both accepted His call and have served together ever since. I thank God infinitely for her life.

All glory be to our Savior and Lord Jesus Christ!

3. THE DREAM CAME TRUE

Pastors Ivan & Marta Villalta

Iglesia Torre de Alabanza & New Life Church, Duarte, CA

Our history

I am originally from Nicaragua. I was born in the city of Managua, and my wife was born in Estelí, another city in this beautiful country. We have a daughter named Karina, who is already married and resides in Seattle, WA.

In addition to being a father and husband, I am also an ordained Assemblies of God pastor. My wife is also involved in ministry and is in the process of getting her license, and very soon, will be in the ordination class. Together, we serve as pastors at Torre de Alabanza and New Life Church in Duarte, CA.

I am a SoCal Network School of Ministry professor and am also privileged to serve as the Hispanic Director of Men's Ministry.

The need for a new life

I met my wife when she was fifteen years old, and from our first meeting, we fell in love. We could say it was love at first sight. After six months, we married and began our journey together, never imagining that God had designed our lives to serve Him.

After six years of marriage, our daughter Karina was born, and she was a gift from God. It was a fantastic event and the fruit of our great love. In the midst of these significant events, marriage, and birth, God was weaving a different plan for us.

At that time, Nicaragua was in the midst of a deep political crisis and needed young people for the army. Unfortunately, in a raid, I was captured and sent to the mountains. At that moment, I felt the urgency in my heart and mind to start a new life far from Nicaragua. So, we decided to flee and seek refuge in a new country that would welcome us: the United States of America. I thought God was leading us to a land where milk and honey flowed, where opportunities abounded, and we knew that with hard work, we could prosper.

Los Angeles, the American dream

In 1988, we finally set foot on the "promised land" and began to immerse ourselves in the culture of our new home. With a suitcase full of dreams, we started a new life far from our homeland but with the certainty of a better future. However, we encountered challenges such as language, economic difficulties, scarcity of resources, and the distance that separated us from our families. What began as a hopeful dream became a struggle for our survival.

In 1992, during the Persian Gulf War, our economy was affected, and unfortunately, I lost my job. The resources I had saved were running out. Despite this, as I have always been an entrepreneur, I believed that my ability and self-confidence would be enough to overcome the situation. However, I was unaware of God's plans for my life, and it was then that Christ began to touch my heart. In the midst of adversity, I fell into a deep depression as I realized that everything, we had fought for, was slipping through my fingers. The American dream seemed to be turning into a nightmare. Nevertheless, God was looking for me. It still resonates in my mind how important I am to God, *"For the Son of Man came to seek and to save that which was lost."* Luke 19:10

In the midst of despair, when I no longer had confidence in myself, I met a friend named Alfredo Somoza, who was a pastor, and visited the watchmaker's shop where I worked.

"Another day, I will go"

On multiple occasions, my friend Alfredo would invite me to his church, but I would make a thousand excuses not to attend and would tell him, "Another day, I will go." So, for nearly a year, I avoided going, convinced that God had no interest in someone like me, full of flaws and insecurities. I felt I had missed the great opportunity to make the great dream I had for my family come true.

By that time, trying to hide my deep depression, I fell into a spiral of drinking more liquor than usual. It became hell for me to have so much responsibility. In the midst of this personal crisis, I received an invitation from a friend to attend his wedding. I thought it would be an excellent opportunity to enjoy a party, eat well, and have a few drinks.

Little did I know that God was knocking on the door of my heart. My wife was suffering from seeing me trapped in depression and wanted to help me but felt helpless. Now I am sure that God's plan was perfect when we joined our lives together. I saw her cry and suffer, but God, with his wisdom and knowledge about the destiny of each one of us, was orchestrating everything behind the events we were living. Who would have thought that a simple invitation to a wedding would open a door to begin a new journey in our lives?

A wedding opens a new beginning

In February 1992, I attended my friend's wedding with my wife, and that day I received the surprise of my life: the officiant of the ceremony was the pastor and friend Alfredo Somoza. His words expounded in the ceremony resonated deep within me, impacting my thoughts and opening a door in my soul. It was the first time I heard the Word of God, and it had a significant effect on my life. During the ceremony, my wife and I looked into each other's eyes and made the decision to attend church the following Sunday. Although we had never attended a Christian church before, we were ready to explore this new experience. At first, I thought it was just another religion, and for the next few months, we went to church every Sunday, but I still wouldn't give up drinking alcohol.

My heart longed to be filled with God's word, but in my mind, I struggled with the idea of making changes in my life. Over the next few months, my depression intensified, and my addiction to alcohol worsened. In those dark moments, I thank God for my pastor because even though I kept making excuses for not going to church, he always had the grace and patience to accept me in those difficult moments of my life.

It was a Sunday in October 1992 when a turning point in my life occurred. After an intense argument with my wife the night before, she confronted me forcefully. She told me that she could no longer stand the life we were living and said these words, "EITHER YOU CHANGE, OR THIS IS OVER BECAUSE WHAT YOU ARE LIVING IS HYPOCRISY." I felt a mixture of emotions, and my initial instinct was to resist because I didn't want to hear that I needed a change in my life.

After the argument that night, I remember I locked myself in my room and did not speak to my wife all night. As I slept, I am sure God calmed my anger, and I woke up in the morning with an unexpected sense of peace. I quickly got ready and told my wife, "Love, we are going to church."

An appointment with God

That Sunday was truly special. The praises filled my heart, and I felt a deep peace. My pastor was preaching, but this time his message had a different impact on me. Although there were many people present, my attention was focused solely on the pastor. As the service progressed, God began to break my life, and I began to cry. I didn't fully understand what was happening, but I knew something significant was happening. My burdens and worries were gone. For the first time, I really understood that God had been searching for me from the moment I was born.

That day, as the pastor gave the altar call to receive Christ as Savior, I raised my hand and walked to the altar. For the first time, I understood that my sin was the reason Jesus had given His life on the cross. I had offended Him through my selfishness and lifestyle. I recognized that it was I who deserved to die on that cross, but Jesus Christ, in His infinite love and sacrifice, had taken my place.

It was a painful experience as I realized the extent of my mistakes and how I had hurt God with my behavior, but that feeling changed in the midst of the time at the altar. I was no longer crying because I had offended God; now, I was crying because God had forgiven me, and I could experience God's mercy and love in my life.

I understood that God is sovereign and that His forgiveness extends to all sinners, but something even deeper resonated in my heart for the first time: God was not only forgiving me but adopting me as his child. That day, I dedicated my life and that of my family to the Lord. It was a transcendental moment in my existence because that Sunday, God marked our destiny and invited us to be part of His great family. We recognized that if God, in His immense love, had forgiven us, then we wanted to dedicate the rest of our lives to serve Him in whatever way He would lead us.

The call to serve the Lord

The day I received Christ, I walked down the aisle with my wife Marta and my daughter Karina, all of us with the desire to renew our commitment to live the new life that God was giving us. That experience completely transformed my spirit and my heart. When I got home, I opened the refrigerator and decided to get rid of all the bottles of alcohol and beer. My friends were the first to hear about what God had done in my life, but unfortunately, they were also the last to hear about it. From that day on, after testifying to them about God's work in my heart, I never saw them again. That night, as I prayed and thanked the Lord for the joy and gladness I was experiencing, I felt a deep burden in my heart for the people who did not yet know Jesus. At that moment, I heard the voice of God saying to me, "You are going to plant a church, and it will be called "Torre de Alabanza."

I shared with my wife that impression I had, but I also confessed to her that it could be just an emotional response to Sunday's experience. From then on, my life took a complete turn, my priorities were transformed, and the purpose of our family was completely redefined. From that day on, we began to live our new life as active members of the Covina Assembly of God Church, where our pastor was in charge of the Hispanic ministry.

Six years of preparation

For the next six years, we continued to attend church faithfully, where my pastor baptized me, and I began to be discipled by him. Although at first, I did not fully understand what discipleship consisted of, I was aware of the great responsibility I had to share with others what God was doing in my life. I became actively involved in different ministry areas within the church: Sunday school, prison ministry, music ministry, as a men's director, and assisting my pastor in whatever needs he had.

My call to ministry did not happen because I heard a voice similar to Moses' in the burning bush, nor because a prophet announced it to me, much less because God had spoken to me directly. Rather, it was through the discipleship of my pastor that I learned to love the church, the bride of Christ. On several occasions, my pastor called me to his office to pray for the brethren and for the church. I saw him suffer and cry on several occasions because of his passion for his service to God. That feeling awakened in me a deep love for the church as well. At that time, I did not know when or how it would happen, but I was sure that I would spend the rest of my life serving the Lord in the church. I was not aware at that time that God's ways are not always our ways. By the time I realized it, I was already completely in love with the church, and that was all that mattered to me. In short, my calling was based on the teaching and example of my pastor. He taught me to have a love for the Lord's church.

The Lord's ways are different from mine

The six years I spent with my pastor was a period of training. I was really happy to be a part of my pastor's life, so much so that I forgot the dream of planting a church. However, God had not forgotten the day He put in my heart the desire to plant a church. In 1998, my pastor had to leave for Seattle, Washington. Suddenly, we found ourselves without a leader and without a church. It was a difficult time, as we did not know what we were going to do.

I did not want to become a pastor as I had witnessed the suffering of my own pastor and thought there might be other ways to serve the Lord. So, if what I loved most was preaching to lost souls, I decided that I would be an evangelist. By that time, I had already attended Bible college and seminary. I was in the middle of my master's degree, and I was still sure that I did not see myself as a pastor of a church. I really did not want to experience the suffering caused by members of a congregation.

I began to contact churches and pastors that I had known through my own pastor, and that was a period of learning and of greater suffering because time and again, I heard the same answers, "We have no offerings to give you for coming to preach." My answer was, "If you will allow me to preach, I myself will be willing to give you offerings." Door after door was closing, but my determination to share the Word was stronger, so I finally began to preach in several churches.

The answer for not pastoring

But then I met a pastor friend who said, "Iván, I was looking for you. I know you don't have a church. Why don't you come to my church and help me preach? I need a preacher for Wednesday and Sunday nights." I thought that was the perfect answer to avoid becoming a pastor. It was preferable to preach without having much responsibility. So, after praying about it, I decided to help this pastor friend. He already had several churches lined up for us to preach. I thought it was the best option for me. During the year I spent with my friend, I experienced a waiting period. I preached in his church and conducted evangelistic campaigns. It was precisely during that time that I realized that I could be serving God but at the same time be in disobedience.

I surrendered my will to the Lord

One unforgettable night, during a campaign at a pastor friend's church in Lake Elsinore, CA, I finally surrendered to the Lord's will. There were many people there that night, and God's presence was palpable. After I finished preaching, everyone came to the altar. There were so many people that I could not pray for each one individually, so we prayed together, and God's anointing came down, causing everyone to fall to the floor (slain in the Spirit). It was amazing to witness how people were saved and healed. God did great miracles on that occasion.

After the campaign ended, I experienced a sense of sin in my heart. I did not understand what was happening. When we got home, my wife and I began to pray, and for the first time, I understood that disobedience was a sin, even when we are serving the Lord. That night I wept bitterly and understood that God did not want me to be an evangelist. God reminded me of the day I received Christ, and He had spoken to me about planting a church.

He had even given me the name of the church. That day I surrendered my will completely to the Lord.

God confirmed His will to me

On Sunday, I arrived at the church where I was helping my friend with the preaching. Right there, God confirmed His call on me. I was in the churchyard, sharing my experience from the night before with a group of men, when my pastor friend saw me among them, and his expression changed, he no longer looked at me as a friend. I noticed something was not right, so I went to his office to tell him about my experience. Before I could say anything to him, he interrupted me and said, "You are like Absalom." I felt very sad and replied, "I don't want to take your kingdom. I came here to tell you that today will be my last service. I am going to plant a church, and believe me, I have not shared this with anyone in your congregation, and I would never call anyone here to leave with me." He then dismissed me with these words, "You will not do well, and you're going to come back here." With mixed feelings of sadness and joy, I left my friend's office; sadness because I wished he would have prayed for us, and joy because I finally knew what God's will was for my life.

We began our church-planting adventure

The following Sunday, we began our church planting adventure in our living room, with only two members: my beloved wife Marta, and my daughter Karina, the two people I love most in my life. For the first four Sundays, I preached to the two of them. My wife would tell me not to speak so loudly as there were only three of us, to which I would reply, "I see a crowd!". When I gave the altar call, my wife and daughter would respond, and I would have the opportunity to minister to them, marking the beginning of our service to God.

The following Sundays, we began to find more people and invited them to meet at our home. After two months, our home was no longer sufficient to accommodate everyone. So, we decided to move the group to a house in the city of Azusa and began to serve in that community.

But I had the feeling that this was not the place where God wanted us. In the next two months, we ran out of space again and had to make another change. A lady who lived in Duarte approached me and said, "Pastor, my house is bigger, and we can meet there. After a few months, we moved to our own community, our own city. The lady also mentioned that she knew other people in Duarte who might be interested in joining our meetings and that her husband, who was not a believer, might have the opportunity to hear the gospel. It was a confirmation from God, as her husband agreed to accept the Lord after the Sunday soccer season was over. On the first Sunday, something incredible happened! The sister's husband was watching a soccer game, and suddenly the TV went off, and he couldn't turn it back on. He said, "I won't be able to watch soccer anymore; the pastor is definitely involved in this." It was funny that every time I turned the corner to his house, the TV went off. That's how we started serving in our community. I realized that establishing the church would take time, as people from Azusa did not want to come to Duarte. So, we made the decision to stay in Duarte and start over.

There was no place for us

We were holding services at Pamela Park. After several attempts to find a place to congregate, we were unsuccessful. Finally, I found the Assemblies of God church, New Life Assembly, where Pastor Glen was the senior pastor. I contacted him to see if he could rent us a room for the winter. He said he would talk to the board and let me know.

Winter was approaching, and the group we had started with had already left because it was so cold and raining. So, I prayed, "Lord, I was obedient to the call you gave me to plant a church. We have no place to meet, and the people are leaving. I will be honest with you, the next Sunday that it rains during our meeting, it will be the last Sunday we will have a service." The weather for the next few Sundays was always cloudy, but it never rained because God was more faithful than I was. I didn't know what to do, so I went to the city of Duarte and asked if they had a room to rent in any of their buildings, to which they told me, "Yes!" By then, I had told the brethren that this next Sunday, we would no longer return to the park or the houses. I told them I didn't know where, but that I trusted that God would open a door.

As I was about to sign for a room in the city of Duarte, at that very moment, I received a call from Pastor Glen, telling me that he had met with the Board of Directors, and they had decided to rent me a room in their church. I put down my pen and quickly made my way to the New Life Duarte church, where I met with Pastor Glen.

November 1999: Torre de Alabanza is born in Duarte

In November 1999, our church, "Torre de Alabanza," was born in the city of Duarte. However, it was not until the year 2000 that we officially inaugurated our church, which God had put on our hearts. For the past twenty-two years, we have pastored this church with love, faith, determination, and the power of God.

When I met Pastor Glen, God put in our hearts a very special affection for each other, similar to the love that existed between friends David and Jonathan, relevant characters in the Bible. At our first meeting, Pastor Glen offered me the use of certain rooms to hold services and asked me what the vision of our church was. I indicated that it was to transform families for Christ. It was interesting to discover that this was exactly the same vision he had. From that day on, a strong friendship, as well as deep love, was formed between us.

I still clearly remember when we walked into the sanctuary, and Pastor Glen said to me, "When your group grows, you can use this." But that Sunday, when we arrived, he looked at me directly and said, "Ivan, don't start in the classrooms; start here in the sanctuary immediately, and for the first eight months, you can use it free of charge." That day, I remembered when God told me we were going to plant a church, which would be called "Torre de Alabanza" (Tower of Praise). That day, my dream came true! I began to weep with joy because it was evident that God was opening doors and creating connections to carry out His will in our lives.

We have planted six daughter churches

During the twenty-two years that we have been pastoring this church, we have had the privilege of planting six daughter churches. We have also trained pastors to raise up other churches in various places in the United States, such as California, Arizona, Miami, and Hawaii, and also in Mexico, Cuba, and Honduras. God has been faithful to the call He placed on our hearts. My wife and I are witnesses of God's growth and fulfillment in our lives.

In 2021, Pastor Glen decided to retire, which led me to assume the role of senior pastor at New Life Assembly of God (English-speaking) as well as continue with Torre de Alabanza (Spanish-speaking). As I move forward in this new responsibility, I continue to marvel at the various ways God surprises me and demonstrates His love and faithfulness to me. All of this is beyond my imagination. I recognize that it is God who calls, empowers, and enables His kingdom to be established in our lives through each church. His power continues to transform the lives of those who congregate and above all, are obedient to God's call.

A new challenge

Today our church is challenged to reach the next generation. To achieve this, we have created a space where they can also experience God's call and the power of His presence. Our church today is no longer just another building but a door of blessing for our community, where we strive to reach and nurture people to be transformed through the power of the Holy Spirit.

Three essential elements to fulfill our vision

1. **Share:**
    a. Transcend the four walls of our church.
    b. To be an instrument of God to share His love to others.
    c. Fulfill the personal mission in our circle of influence, between (eight to fifteen people).

2. Connect:
a. Create spaces in which new believers can participate.
b. Develop strategies to integrate each believer into existing teams.
c. Build bridges of friendship to counteract the enmity that exists in this world.

3. Complement:
a. Create teams in which we complement each other, instead of competing with each other.
b. Establish a discipleship that is reproducible, so that more people can be formed and trained.
c. Develop a system of influence based on trust.
d. Desire that Torre de Alabanza continue to train people who can establish meaningful connections with future generations.

4. EVERYTHING WILL BE ALL RIGHT

Pastor Mario Arguedas

Calvary Church Assemblies of God, South Gate, CA

Born in Costa Rica

My parents were an excellent example; even though they were not believers, they instilled in us the fear of God, respect for others, respect for adults, and to think and help the needy.

We were a large family, but we were blessed to have hard-working parents. My father owned a seafood restaurant which, thank God, was thriving and allowed them to support a family of five sons and three daughters. In total, there were ten of us in the household, counting my parents.

We all attended school and were very dedicated to our studies, until one sunny afternoon, on the way home from school, something unexpected happened that changed my life. Several of us were walking, playing, and joking around on the cobblestone streets of our neighborhood when a tragic accident occurred. An intoxicated man was driving a motorcycle and hit me. I fell on the loose stones and bounced off one of them. When I woke up, I was in the hospital with a severe head injury and a broken leg.

That blow to the head had a big impact on my life. It damaged a nerve in my brain, and I lost 50% of my memory. To this day, I remember absolutely nothing from when I was twelve years old or younger, which hindered my ability to study as I wished. Over the years, I have also faced difficulties in writing, as my hand tends to fall asleep after only a few minutes. But I thank God for His plans for me and His constant help in my life. "I know the plans I have for you, for your welfare and not for your evil, to give you a future full of hope. I, the Lord, affirm it." Jeremiah 29:11 DHH94I

There is no doubt that, for those of us who love God, everything we experience here on earth has a purpose, and furthermore, everything contributes to our good, even if at the time, we don't understand it.

If you are going through a difficult or tragic situation, trust in God and remember that His plans are for your well-being. Hold on to His faithfulness and discover it through the holy book, the Bible.

From an Adventure to a Blessing

Around 1981, my cousin invited me to go with him to the United States, specifically to Miami. The initial plan was to work on a cruise ship, earn some money, and then return to Costa Rica. However, as I said before, God's plans are very different from what we think or even plan. We determined to leave Costa Rica and embark on the journey to the United States. Since we were in no hurry, we decided to travel overland to see the other Central

American countries. We both had U.S. visas, which allowed us to arrive directly and legally in Miami, but first, we wanted to explore other countries.

We started the trip with many tears from my parents, and after saying goodbye, we set off on our journey to the north. We thought we had enough money with us, but sometimes at eighteen, one often miscalculates and unfortunately, that is what happened to my cousin Neftali and me. I remember we had a few drinks to avoid thinking about the family we were leaving behind and mistakenly, and according to our perception at the time, to feel more secure.

As the days went by, our drinking increased. It was no longer one or two drinks but more and more, and the money we brought was running out. When we arrived in México, we liked the country and took the opportunity to visit many places. We felt confident and like we owned the world, but our goal was still to get to Miami. My cousin, Neftali, had contacts so we could apply for a job on a cruise ship. We had previously agreed between both of us that before going to Miami, we would stay a few days in Los Angeles to see some famous places. We thought we "had it all figured out," according to us.

We faced a very serious problem

After two weeks of travel from Costa Rica, we arrived in Tijuana and headed for the San Isidro border to cross into the United States. We felt confident, just as we had been in the countries we had just visited without any problems. However, at this point, we had very little money because we had wasted it without considering the consequences it could bring us. So, when we arrived at the border, we had our passports and visas all in order, but we faced a serious problem.

Upon arrival with the immigration officer, he asked us how long we planned to stay in Los Angeles. We both replied that we would be there for two weeks. Up to that point, everything was going well; there were no problems. But when the officer asked us how much money we had for the trip, suddenly, we remembered all

61

the liquor we had consumed. We only had $150.00 between my cousin and me. When we told the officer how much money we had, he just laughed. He kindly informed us that this amount would only last us four days, as we would have to pay for room and board during our stay. But in addition to the little money we were carrying, we could not produce evidence of a return ticket to our country. As a result, we were denied entry into the United States. They stamped our passports with a "no entry to the United States" indication, which was more than enough to make us feel defeated, discouraged, penniless, and alone in a place like Tijuana.

There is always a kind person willing to help

In Tijuana, someone offered to cross us illegally into the United States for the amount of $250.00 each, but obviously, it was not possible to accept the offer, as we did not have enough money. After six hours, that same person possibly took pity on us and offered to help us cross the border for the amount of money we had at that time, but we would owe him the rest of the money.

We talked to this person again and finally agreed to give him the $150.00, with the promise to pay him the rest when we got a job. He agreed, which was a great relief, and after two attempts, we made it across the border to Gardena, California. There we met Ulises Quezada, a Costa Rican native and believer in Christ. To this day, I thank God for Ulises' life. His help was invaluable to us. He opened the doors of his home, and since we were fellow countrymen, he took us into his care. He took us to church, discipled us, and gave us immense support. I want to thank you, Ulises, for having such a generous heart and for helping others in this way.

My Walk as a Believer

My good friend Ulises began to talk to us about the things of God, and that awakened in us a great interest. However, we were not completely convinced, especially when it came to renouncing our religion. Our faith was something sacred, and we were not ready to give it up, at least that's what we thought at the time, but as I mentioned before, God's plans are very different from the plans of men. After attending church for several months, we witnessed the love of God, and the attention we received from the Christian community attracted us. *"With cords of men I drew them, with cords of love; and I was unto them as they that lift up the yoke from off their neck and set meat before them."* -Hosea 11:4 NKJV1960.

Especially in my life, this desire to know more about God grew. My cousin Neftali was determined to leave for Miami because of the friends and job possibilities he had there. He told me, "I am going, and when I have enough money, I will send for you to join me." Our friend and compatriot Ulises warned him, "Don't go! God can bless you here!" However, my cousin did not listen and left for Miami. To my surprise, he never asked me to come, and after three months, I received a letter from him asking me to deposit three thousand dollars so he could post bail to get out of an immigration detention center. But where would I get three thousand dollars if I only worked one or two days a week? Finally, my cousin was deported back to Costa Rica. It hurt me a lot not to be able to help him. Now I felt alone without any family and far from my country. It was then that I decided to give my life to God. I opened my heart and accepted Jesus as my personal Savior. I want to tell you that giving my life to Jesus was the best decision of my life.

God is faithful

Since I gave my heart to Jesus, I have witnessed many miracles in my life. In 1986, an amnesty was granted to all illegal immigrants living in the United States, and thanks to God's goodness, I had an orderly life and no criminal record, so this facilitated my immigration procedures, and everything went very well. I am sure that God allowed me to have everything in order. I thank God that that same year I was able to return to my beautiful country, Costa Rica, to visit my family and share with them the love of God.

In 1990 I took the oath to become a citizen of the United States of America. I love this great nation, although, in my heart, I will always be a "Tico" (diminutive used to name Costa Ricans). I thank

God for my two beautiful daughters, Elizabeth and Ruth, and for their husbands, Josué and Manuel. And, of course, not forgetting my two granddaughters, Emma and Joanna. In 2022, God allowed us all to go on vacation together to Costa Rica, and for the first time, my granddaughters ate "Gallo Pinto" (a traditional dish from Costa Rica and other Central American countries), and they loved it. We enjoyed a lovely family time together.

Called to the Ministry

In 1990, the Lord led me to work in a church in Lomita, CA. As a maintenance man, I had the responsibility of ensuring the cleanliness and good condition of the building, ensuring the sanitation of the restrooms, changing damaged lights, taking care of transportation, and picking up the mail. This was the job that helped me discover my calling to ministry and to realize God's plans for my life. At that time, no one believed in my potential, not even myself, especially when it came to serving God and the ministry.

When my pastor would ask someone to share a testimony, read scripture or sing a song to start the service, I would come late or hide under the pews because of my shyness. I was very afraid to speak in public and to share my faith openly. But I discovered that when we are in God's plans, there is no escape.

Brother or friend, if you find yourself feeling uneasy about a calling God is giving you, don't be afraid. Trust that God will enable you to fulfill what He is calling you to do. Just obey!

The maintenance work in that church gave me the opportunity to meditate, reflect and pray as I had time to do so while performing my duties. In addition, the pastors there were very kind and full of God's presence. On several occasions, the senior pastor found me praying or preaching to the empty pews of the church while vacuuming. I remember one particular time when he saw me in the pulpit preaching to the empty benches. No one was there, but for me at that moment, the church was full of people listening to my message.

The pastor had been watching me for months, although I didn't know it. Nevertheless, God knew perfectly well my situation and what was going on in my life. After a few months, the pastor unexpectedly asked me if I knew anyone who would be willing to start a work or church in that building, for Spanish-speaking people, since all the services were conducted in English. Although I did not know anyone who fit that description, I decided to mention the situation to my own pastor of the congregation I attended regularly. The service at this church was in Spanish. When I told him about this opportunity, he indicated that if he found someone interested, he would let me know.

Inside me, I felt the call of God

Several years went by, and it seemed that no concrete opportunity presented itself regarding the call of God that I perceived in my heart. In 1994, I received unexpected news at work. I was informed that a pastor from Tijuana was coming to establish a Hispanic work. Unfortunately, the pastor never arrived. The senior pastor of the church where I worked came and asked me explicitly if I would be willing to establish a Hispanic work in the building. He indicated that there was plenty of space available at the site, which offered a unique opportunity to start a Hispanic congregation.

Even though I felt a call from God to serve Him, my immediate response was, "I am not qualified to be a pastor." After six or eight months, I was asked once again about starting a Hispanic church.

At their insistence, I then decided to talk to the pastor of the church where I was congregating, but unfortunately, he seemed to ignore my words, which made me doubt even more if this was really for me. I said to myself, "Maybe this is not what God wants for me."

They persisted once again in consulting me about the possibility of starting the Hispanic church, and with many fears and doubts, I finally said, "Yes!" Honestly, at the time, I figured it would be a small group of about six people.

Finally, in 1995, after much prayer, we started the Hispanic work, and to my surprise, God began to send many people. My first message was based on these verses that I will never forget: *"And Jabez was more illustrious than his brethren, whom his mother called Jabez, saying Because I bare him in sorrow. And Jabez called upon the God of Israel, saying, O that Thou wouldest bless me, and enlarge my land, and that Thy hand might be with me, and that Thou wouldest deliver me from evil, that I should not be hurt. And God granted him what he asked."* 1 Chronicles 4:9-10.

After that sermon, where there were only four people present, I sensed a strong desire to study theology. I wished that my pastor, where I was a member, would have oriented me, or trained me, but it was not to be. So, I began reading books, researching different institutes, and attending seminars. Eventually, we became the Spanish department of the Assemblies of God Church in Lomita, CA.

I became actively involved in the SoCal Network of the Assemblies of God, participating in retreats, seminars, and training. At that time, there was no School of Ministry as there is today, but I began to study by correspondence at Global University, Berean School, in Springfield, MO. By the grace of God, I persevered and graduated. Today, I am an ordained pastor and am blessed to lead a sovereign church.

Missionaries Richard and Janice Larson

All this would not have been possible without the help of missionaries Richard and Janice Larson. Brother Richard, in particular, played a fundamental role in my process to become a certified credentialed minister. Taking classes and sitting for exams required extraordinary effort on my part. I tried my best and recognized the grace of God that was manifesting in my life. After a few years, Brother Richard asked me if I was ready to take the next step and become a licensed minister. I confess that at first, I was scared and tried to avoid it since it implied a greater commitment to study and dedication. Besides, as I mentioned at the beginning, I had always found it difficult to concentrate. However, I decided to face that fear, and once again, as before, I overcame it. Brother Richard was a pivotal key in the process of obtaining my credentials. "Thank you, Brother Richard, for your support and for giving me the necessary push and encouraging me to believe in myself and my abilities.

After several years, Brother Richard presented a group of pastors with the challenge of taking classes and taking the exams to obtain ordination as ministers. I must admit that initially, I made excuses and showed resistance. I felt reluctant, negative, and even conformist. I already had my church, participated in section wide events, and attended annual pastors' meetings. I believed that I was already "ordered" (in every sense of the word), but the reality was that I was disordered.

I accepted Brother Richard's challenge, and today I thank God for taking that step. During the whole process, I was able to experience the help of the Holy Spirit as He guided me in my studies. Brother Richard showed great patience and support at all times, and finally, I was able to reach my goal. It is wonderful to experience that when we are in God's plans, nothing can stop us. I remember the story of Jonah, who tried to run away from God's will. However, God pursued him and used various means to make Jonah obey His call and fulfill His purpose in him. *"The LORD will accomplish His purpose in me; Your lovingkindness, O LORD, endures forever; Do not forsake the work of Your hands."* Psalms 138:8 ESV1960

It was time to leave the nest

After many years of being a Spanish department of Lomita A/G Church in Lomita, the American pastor informed us that it was time to leave the nest and start looking at options to move. By then, the church already had some savings for when our moving day came. We started looking at church buildings and ran into different obstacles. Many of these buildings did not have enough parking for cars. Others did not have offices or classrooms for youth and children's classes. I must admit that I liked some of the buildings because they were close to where many families in our congregation lived. Unfortunately, some of them did not have permits to operate as a church.

But the biggest obstacle was that we did not meet the requirements of any bank to be approved for a loan, since our plan as a congregation was to purchase property. During that transition period, many painful situations accumulated. Now I can talk about those circumstances because I am now healthy and can talk about it with a heart free of anger.

While I was busy looking for a new building, I was also experiencing constant pressure from the church where we were staying, as we were regularly asked about the situation and the date of our move. My eldest daughter, Elizabeth, was busy preparing for her wedding. At the same time, we were going through a very difficult family situation as my father became ill and passed away. In addition, I was receiving letters from banks denying our loan applications. I also went through a divorce, which, given the way events unfolded, was extremely painful. God put me through the fire, but even in the midst of the trials, God did not abandon me; He was by my side and continues to be there. Thank God, the entire congregation offered me great support during this painful process.

But it was also a time when I got closer to God than ever before. I would get up at five in the morning and literally run to church, throw myself on the floor to pray, cry, write, and read the Bible. One early morning, I felt God's love so strongly, and as if with a whisper in my ear, He said, "Everything will be all right!" That phrase was repeated over and over again, "Everything will be all right!" At that moment, I decided to believe and receive that word in my heart, which became a balm for my soul. I got up from the place where I was prostrate, and to this day, I can affirm that the healing balm led me to believe in God for great things, and I have seen it become real in my life.

May 2017 – Calvary Church moves to South Gate, CA

Two months after that personal experience with God, many doors began to open. First, I experienced healing in my soul.

Secondly, the bank approved us for a loan to buy a building. Third, the house that had been on the market for more than a year finally sold. God began to work miracles, and the signatures we needed for the church building loan came through. The building we are currently in was the one we were able to acquire at that time. We began to renovate the building, including the kitchen hall and the sanctuary.

God does marvelous works, and through the dark valleys of life, He tests us in our faith and in the attitude of our hearts. *"And we know that all things work together for good to them that love God, to them who are the called according to His purpose."* Romans 8:28 NKJV1960

To the glory of God, May 2022 marks five years since we moved from Lomita to South Gate, and we have experienced growth in our church. For that, we thank God! We are committed to our community and provide weekly food assistance to over 100 families. We hold a general open-air service each month, and God continues to add those who will be saved, as mentioned in Acts 2:47. We have two services on Sundays and one on Fridays, in addition to other activities during the week. I say again that God has been good and will continue to be good.

We continue to move forward

Our church has been very generous, which has allowed us to support missionaries around the world. Despite facing obstacles, we are experiencing victory.

If at any time you feel stuck or if your dreams have not yet been fulfilled, don't be discouraged. Keep trusting, praying, and planning all at the same time. If you have been chosen by God, rest assured that he will fulfill His purpose in you, because God is faithful. Allow God to fight for you and rest in his promises. *"Do not worry, for the Lord will fight for you."* Exodus 14:14 DHH94I

A very special thanks to Sister Janice Larson for considering me in this book and for all her hard missionary work in several countries in Latin America. You, Brother and Sister Larson have been a great blessing to many of us, who at one time doubted our abilities, and were an inspiration to respond to God's call. May God, our Lord, reward you abundantly.

My prayer is that by reading this book, many brothers and sisters in the faith will believe that they can achieve their dreams by serving the King.

In the love of Jesus Christ,
Pastor Mario Arguedas

5. I DON'T THINK I'M MADE FOR THIS

Pastors Agustín & Griselda Pérez

Rapto Divino Church, Fresno, CA and Madera, CA

We are from Oaxaca, Mexico

Agustin: I was born September 4, 1970, and am from Oaxaca, Mexico. I come from a traditional Catholic family. My father was very religious in terms of Catholicism. I am the last in the family to be baptized in Catholicism. We were nine siblings, and I was fourth in the line of siblings.

When I was twelve years old, I left elementary school and began to have difficulties in my relationship with my parents, which led me to completely withdraw from the church. During my time in high school, I began to engage in inappropriate behavior. At the age of sixteen, I met my future wife.

Griselda: I was born September 13, 1970, and am also from Oaxaca, Mexico. My childhood was lonely. My father was in the United States, and I didn't get to know him until I was eight or nine years old. My siblings and I were in Mexico with my mother. We were eleven siblings, and I was fourth.

I met my husband in 1987. He used to take me to dances and led a very worldly life. In 1988 we got married in Mexico, and about three years later, in 1991, I met and accepted Jesus Christ as my Savior. Although I come from a Catholic background, I had never experienced the love and salvation of Jesus Christ. Since making my profession of faith, I remain firmly rooted in Him.

We lived a tough life of disputes, fights, and abuse

Agustin: I came to the United States in 1988 and arrived directly in Fresno because I had some relatives who helped us to come here. I started working in Fresno while Griselda, my wife, stayed one more year in Mexico.

Griselda: When my husband moved to the United States, he began to live a disorderly life and became utterly lost. He was messed up in Mexico, but when he arrived in the United States, he became totally corrupted. Therefore, we decided to separate, and in 1990, I left Mexico and went to San José, CA, to be with my family. We were separated for a while.

Agustin: My parents had accepted the Lord, and even though they didn't know much about reading, they preferred to go to church instead of watching TV. Their decision to serve the Lord was a great help to us. My wife and I were now living with them, and they always encouraged us to attend church and seek God.

I worked in construction, specifically installing roofs for houses. Our married life was extremely difficult, full of conflicts, fights, and abuse. Without the fear of God, both Griselda and I were horrible people.

Griselda: My husband didn't want to go to church, but my in-laws insisted that we go.

Agustin: Despite being immersed in many situations that led me down a bad path, without fear of God, in 1993, I made the decision to attend the church where my mother, father, and wife went. It was there that I had my encounter with God and experienced salvation.

A new love is reborn

When the Lord saved me is when marriage really began for Griselda and me. We experienced a completely new freshness and renewal. A new love was reborn between us.

We had a bad experience in the small church where we were attending. As we read the Bible and grew in the knowledge of God, we began to notice that this church shared teachings that were against biblical doctrine. We witnessed psychological and spiritual abuse by some people. We felt belittled and criticized, even called ignorant. The Word of God was not often used, and instead, it was combined with humanistic approaches and psychologies for personal gain.

I remember expressing to my wife that what we were witnessing did not agree with the teachings of the Bible. We decided to talk to the pastors, express our gratitude, and ask God to lead us to another church.

We started praying at my parent's house since we were living with them at the time. On Wednesdays, my mom, my brothers, my wife, and I would get together to pray, asking, "Lord, lead us to a church we can attend. We don't want to be disconnected."

Others started coming to pray

Other people started coming to join us in prayer and expressed their appreciation and interest. They wanted to know when we would meet again to pray. Over time, more people joined, and in about three months, we were meeting with around twenty-five to thirty people. We were inexperienced and did not know what God's call to serve meant, nor did we know for sure what a church was.

I decided to talk to a pastor, not the one who had hurt us, to explain the situation and seek advice. After listening to me, he said, "Look, Agustin, if I were selfish, I would tell you to come to my church, bring all these people, and help me with the youth, but you know Agustin, these people are not looking at me as their leader, they are looking at you, and God is calling you to serve Him, and you must do it." At that statement, I was astonished because I did not know how to speak in public, nor how to dress properly. I really knew nothing about serving God. This pastor very kindly offered me his help and explained to me what it meant to serve God. I told him that I didn't think I was cut out for this work. But he insisted again and again and told me, "Follow Him, follow Him! I will introduce you to an American pastor in whose church you could lead the Hispanic department." However, I still had doubts about being able to perform this service for the Lord.

The North Fresno Assemblies of God church contacted us, welcomed us with open arms, and we started holding services in the dining hall on Sundays, Tuesdays, and Fridays. To our surprise, people began to attend.

We had the leading of the Holy Spirit

Agustin: For someone who knows nothing about being a pastor, it was a mixture of emotions. My focus was on my family, my work, and the routine of the whole world. Now, without any experience, I also had to attend to the responsibilities of the church, like preaching, general administration, and how to deal with people.

Thank God I had learned something from what happened in the other church. I began to understand what the service meant, but still, everything was new. In the previous meetings, people were crying, some were falling in the Spirit, evil spirits were manifesting, and others were making salvation decisions. All of this made me nervous, and I wondered, "What is going on here?" I had never experienced anything like this, but with God's grace and the leading of the Holy Spirit, my wife and I began to taste the ministry and learn what we were to do.

My experience of a call to serve

Griselda: In the beginning, my involvement in the church was limited. I mainly helped by driving people home after services. I was focused on my children and was not very involved in direct service in the church.

There was an obstacle in my life to serve, and it had as a background something that the pastor of the previous church had told me regarding a dream I had. He told me that my dream of being called to the ministry was just the result of indigestion, from having eaten too much the night before!

He added that the call to serve was exclusively for my husband and that I had nothing to do with it since, according to his criteria, the ministry was not for women. Although I respected my pastor very much, those words affected me negatively and remained engraved in my mind. When my husband and I started in the pastorate, he asked me to pray for the women in the church, but those words of the pastor kept echoing in my mind, and I told myself that this was not for me, that the calling was only for my husband.

So, it continued for many years until, one day, my husband became ill. A spiritual weariness set in, and I became angry with my husband because he prayed so fervently for the people. It's OK, but what about our family? It is good that he prays, but not that much. Because my husband was sick, people would then come to our house looking for him, asking for the pastor, and I would tell them

75

that he was not available and would return at a specific time. But when he came back, he simply needed to rest and could not pray for the people at that time.

So, I took the initiative to ask people what they needed, and they began to share their problems with me. I began to feel the burden in my heart, I felt compassion and the pain of the people, and God began to work in me as I saw their needs. I now understood my husband and why he even cried when he prayed for other people's needs. It was because his heart was full of love, and he wanted to help others. It was at that moment that I felt a strong calling on my life to serve the Lord and decided to study for ministerial credentials.

We left North Fresno Church

We stayed in the American church until 1996. Our departure from North Fresno was not because of any conflict or problem we had, but because we felt that God was using the pastor to move us into something new. When we first met at North Fresno Church, the place where we were meeting was very small, and we didn't have enough space, but the Pastor said to me, "Augustin, move to the sanctuary and have the services at different times than mine."

So, we followed his advice until one day, Pastor told me, "Look, Agustin, if I keep you here, you will not grow. It would be like the young man who stays at home and does not experience his independence and his own way." So, he suggested that we look for a place of our own to rent. I agreed with the idea and said, "That's perfect. That seems fine with me." Although the church was generating income, up to that point, all the finances were going directly to North Fresno and staying there.

We rented a facility for the church

Then we rented a place and moved, started taking care of our own finances, and became independent. We were no longer a department but a group/church. We looked for a name and decided to call it Rapto Divino. Eventually, the opportunity arose to join another group, but we decided to stay with the Assemblies of God.

That's when we met our beloved missionary Brother Harry Bartel. I believe it was with him that we went to the Assemblies of God SoCal Network office in Irvine. He was a great help to us. We began to understand our position with the Assemblies of God. We obtained the Bylaws Manual and received greater support from the SoCal Network for the church.

"Give this place to Agustin!"

We began to grow some more and found it necessary to move to another location. As we continued to grow, we began to pray for a building for our church. We had a desire to purchase a theater that was available when we met Pastor Jesse Alvarez. I had already seen him on several occasions, and one day he said to me, "Agustin, my church is at 3707 E. Laurite, and we have a building that we are going to leave because we are moving to north Fresno. I am praying to God to know what to do with this building, and God has spoken to me three times to give it to you." "Really, pastor?" I was amazed! Brother Alvarez didn't know me very well, but God had clearly indicated to him, "Give this place to Agustin." "Pastor Jesse, I believe it's from God because we are praying to find something," I asked Jesse then what was his final proposition.

Jesse explained, "Look, Agustin, God has led me to pass the building on to you. Here's what we're going to do: come and continue paying the monthly mortgage payments; we've already paid our share, and the modifications we made are in good shape. I don't want anything in return, just keep paying. Apply for a loan through the bank that is associated with the Assemblies of God, and if you are approved for the loan, the building will be yours."

That's how in 2000, we moved to where we are now. And it continues with the same church name, "RAPTO DIVINO."

We began to study for credentials

In the year 2000, we met the Larsons and began to receive their help. Brother Richard started to insist on my studying. He asked me if I had credentials, to which I responded that I had a provisional credential that is granted when I began to affiliate until I complete my studies and obtain the definitive credential. Due to my lack of experience, I was not studying in a formal way, until one day, Brother Larson told me in a direct way, "Agustín, the only way you will obtain credentials is if you study." So, I started studying at Berean Global University from home to get the first level of credentials. He went on to explain the levels of credentials. For the other levels, Griselda and I traveled 500 miles round trip to attend Berean classes two days a month at the Network offices in Irvine, which were taught by Brother Larson. We finally completed the Ordination level!

My health was deteriorating

Agustin: In the midst of all that we were experiencing in the ministry, I began to face problems with my kidneys. At first, I didn't understand what was happening to me. I thought that maybe I had not been wise in my dietary choices. But then it became clear that I had a major deterioration in my kidneys. My kidneys were only functioning at 5% or 8%. I began to experience symptoms of fatigue, and my ability to tolerate food decreased. Although I was not in pain, I felt extremely tired. Until one day in the afternoon, I lay down on the couch and felt like I would not wake up. I had lost a lot of weight and had no appetite, and my wife said, "Let's go to the hospital because this is not normal at all."

We went to the hospital, and they did an analysis. The doctor informed me, "Agustin, your kidneys are no longer functioning properly. They are not filtering properly, and you are poisoned. If we don't start dialysis, you could die." It was a hard blow to receive that news, but we had to make the decision to start dialysis, and happily, I began to feel better.

When one visits a hospital, it is usually to share the gospel of Christ, pray for the sick, and give them words of hope. But now, lying in the hospital bed, I needed help, words of hope, and prayer. I needed someone to tell me, "Don't worry, everything is going to be all right."

There was an American man there whom I didn't know, and he didn't know me. Even though I didn't speak much English, he came up to me and said, "I have a word for you from God. He says that the job you have is a life-saving job. You have many spiritual children, and even though you are going through this, it is just a process, and it will soon be over."

That's when I understood that God had placed this man there to pastor me at this time. Everything he told me turned out to be the truth.

I knew everything would be all right

So, I gathered my strength, nurtured my hope, and knew that everything was going to be okay. My spirits rose again, and I declared, "Whatever comes, I know I'm not going to die. I know I'm going to get through it." And I did.

I started dialysis sessions, and the doctor informed me that they would put my name on the waiting list for a transplant, but we had to understand that the wait could take four to eight years. At that moment, I experienced a very strong emotional impact and had to accept it.

We went to a doctor who performed an analysis and informed us that if my wife was compatible, the waiting time would obviously be shorter. Once the blood tests were done, we were informed that my wife was a match. The doctor looked at me and said, "Agustín, I see you as a very positive man. I think you have something I don't understand, and I want to apologize for taking your wife's blood. I think you deserve a transplant, and if you are willing, since we are going to operate on you to place a kidney, we would also transplant your pancreas since you are diabetic, and you are at risk in that sense as well. Both the kidney and the pancreas will be from the same donor. The risks are high, with a 50% chance of survival and a 50% chance of death. It is up to you to decide. I replied, "Well, yes, let's do it!"

I think I will have the transplant in nine months

When I left the clinic, I said to my wife, "Just as a woman carries her child in her womb for nine months, I declare right now that in nine months, I will receive my transplant! And sure enough, at nine months, I was receiving my kidney and pancreas. God is mighty! Now, years later, my health is excellent and back to normal. I take medication, trust in God, take care of myself, and have no problems.

The family works together

It is a great blessing to have a wife who has also been called to the service of God and the church. She is often called "the pastor's wife" or in Spanish, "pastora," but really, Griselda is a pastor. She has credentials and is a great help to me. I believe that half of what is accomplished in the church is due to her dedication. She preaches, teaches, and provides valuable assistance with paperwork and computer work. If I have to be absent, I don't worry because I know she will take care of everything as if I were present. She also helps with the ladies, teachers, and children. We have two churches, and she preaches in both. Her real delight is teaching and seeing how people learn and grow.

We have two churches: Rapto Divino in Fresno, CA, and Rapto Divino in Madera, CA. In addition, we travel to Mexico to preach in various places. My wife and I are considering the possibility, with the support and backing of our churches, of starting something in Mexico. Although it is not yet official, the possibility exists. It is God who is directing our steps in that way.

We have four children: Genesis, Isaí, Agustín Eli, and Eliel, who give us such valuable help in the ministry! They are all well-prepared, and some of them have graduated in music studies in

Hillside, Australia, and also in Christ for the Nations in Texas; we thank God for them.

The greatest satisfaction in serving God

We are convinced that the greatest reward or satisfaction a pastor can experience is to see a person who was completely destroyed, fragmented into pieces, with his life headed for damnation, being regenerated by God to the point where they begin to preach and evangelize, leading a completely new life. This kind of testimony motivates us to keep going and urges us to say, "Wow, let's go for more!".

Everything is overcome with God's help

There are challenges in serving God that can be painful, but we believe they are part of being followers of Christ, who is the founder of the church. If the Savior of the world faced trials and struggles, it is to be expected that we will also face them. It is natural for us to have illusions and expectations. However, when God tells us, "You are going to serve me and do what I tell you, not what you want," we understand that the difficult challenges that arise in ministry can be overcome with God's help. We learn to leave them behind, overcome them and move on because we trust that in the end, scripture teaches us that we are not to trust in man, but in God.

We want to thank God for allowing us to serve Him and we also thank the Assemblies of God for the support they give us. We thank God for where we are now and for the coverage we receive. Our desire is that God will continue to help us be faithful to Him at all times.

Legacy for the next generations

Over the years, we have made improvements to the roof and the part where the platform and altar are located, seeking to modernize the space. We also expanded the space for the children by installing double-wide trailers. We plan to continue making improvements gradually.

This has been a good place for us, but we also have a vision for the future that will be fulfilled over time. Before the Lord calls us into His presence, or it is time for us to retire, we want to leave a legacy for the next generations.

6. "BUT GOD"

Pastor Adelita Garza

Iglesia Puente de Vida & Bridge of Life Church, Santa Paula, CA

But God had another plan

My name is Adelita Garza. I was born and raised in the small town of Othello, Washington. My father was born in Nuevo Leon, Mexico, and immigrated to the United States when he was eighteen years old, settling in Washington State. On the other hand, my mother was born in the state of Texas and moved to Washington with her parents when she was eight years old. It was in Washington where my parents met, married, and still reside in the small town of my childhood and adolescence.

My life did not turn out exactly as I had imagined. My childhood and teenage dream was to become a successful computer engineer who would live in wealth. But God had another plan for my life. I would have never dreamed this life for myself, but I'm so thankful that God did. It hasn't always been easy, but I am convinced it's the best life I could be living.

I wanted something different for my life

I am one of thirteen siblings and have been blessed with a large family. I started working in the fields at the early age of ten. As members of a large family, we quickly learned how to work together to make ends meet. Working under the hot sun cutting asparagus, topping onions, and picking strawberries and cherries was hard for a young kid like me and my siblings while we were still children. When I was thirteen, I also worked at a restaurant called Steak House. In the mornings, from 5:30 am to 8:00 am, I worked in the fields and then went to school from 8:30 am to 3:00 pm., After school, I would go to the Steak House to work some more. I would usually leave work at the Steak House around 8 pm with just enough time to do my homework and then go to bed at 10 pm. The next day, I would get up early to repeat the cycle again. I am grateful to my father, who instilled in us a strong work ethic, even though it involved a lot of hard work.

I wanted something different for my life. I often dreamed of going to college, becoming a computer engineer, and never working under the hot sun again. This dream became my yearning and inspired me to perform well academically. To the glory of God, I became the salutatorian of my high school graduating class. I was determined to make a better life for myself and, consequently, for my family.

It was a miracle!

I grew up in a Christian home. I had wonderful parents who loved Jesus. There were family dysfunctions, as you can imagine a family of thirteen children would have, but we also came to know Jesus and His incredible love. I personally accepted Jesus and knew He was real after experiencing a miraculous healing at the age of eight. I will never forget that day.

The school nurse had told me two weeks earlier that I needed eyeglasses. Later, my mom took me to the optometrist to have my eyes checked. The doctor confirmed that I needed glasses and prescribed them. As my mom and I walked out of the optometrist's office, I remember looking at her with tears in my eyes and saying, "I don't want to wear glasses!" My mom insisted that I needed them. I continued to cry and tell her, "Please, Mom, I don't want to wear them!" My mom told me, "If you pray and ask Jesus to heal you, and He does, you won't need to wear them." For the next few weeks, I prayed with child-like faith. I prayed every day. I couldn't wait to go back to the doctor's office.

The day of my doctor's appointment arrived. As I walked into the office, I told my mother that I didn't need glasses. It was our turn to be seen by the doctor. The doctor came out with my glasses and said, "Here you go, Adelita, your new glasses." I looked at the doctor and said, "I don't need them!" He smiled at me and then looked at my mom. She kindly asked the doctor if he could recheck my eyes again because I was convinced Jesus had healed me. The doctor generously agreed. That day I walked out of the optometrist's office without glasses. It was a miracle! A miracle that assured me of Jesus' saving grace, and I have never looked back. And to the honor and glory of God, I still have 20/20 vision today.

God surprised me again!

Another personal miracle that marked my life occurred when I was thirteen years old. God healed me of Scoliosis. The doctor had already informed my parents and me that I would need to wear a back brace for one year, otherwise I would walk hunched over at a very young age. I remember crying because I didn't want my friends to see me in a brace. I was embarrassed just thinking I would be the only teenager walking the high school hallways with a back brace.

But God surprised me once again! One day after school, I went to the athletic club owned by some relatives. When I arrived, I went to a corner, sat down, and fell into depression, thinking about what life would be like with a brace. I imagined that my classmates and friends would make fun of me and ignore me. It felt like a nightmare. However, I didn't know that God had something great in store for me.

That same day, a professional bodybuilder who was also a traveling evangelist walked into the Athletic Club. He saw me in the corner, depressed, and came over to ask me what was wrong. I told him about my situation, and he looked at me and asked, "Do you want to be healed?" I immediately replied, 'Yes!' Then he asked me, "Can I pray for you?" And I repeated, "Yes!" Together we headed to one of the offices. He asked me more questions and soon discovered that one side of my hip was higher than the other. That caused one leg to be shorter than the other.

The evangelist directed me to sit on the floor and show him my situation. As I did so, I could see that one leg was about two inches shorter than the other. He then asked me if I believed God could heal me. I knew that God could heal me, and I said, "Yes!" The evangelist began to pray in the name of Jesus that my leg would grow and line up with the other leg. As he prayed, I began to feel my leg grow. It was amazing! It was a miracle! It was the supernatural power of God manifesting before my eyes.

When I finally stood up from the cold floor, my hips were aligned, my legs were the same length, and my back straightened. I never had to wear a back brace. I had always believed in God's ability to heal me, but I never imagined witnessing it with my own eyes. It was an incredible experience, and I am thankful for the miracle God worked in my life. It was amazing!

God had a different plan for me

My faith in Christ continued to grow in my teenage years. Youth group services, camps, and events were a fundamental part of my spiritual growth. Growing up in a Pentecostal church where altar calls were given, and the fire of the Holy Spirit was experienced taught me to be passionate about God. I desired to honor and serve God to the best of my ability. As I excelled in my academics in high school, I believed I would serve God as a computer engineer.

BUT GOD! God had a different plan for me. He had another dream and purpose for my life. It all began to become clear at the altar of a youth camp when I was sixteen years old. Although I had attended multiple camps before, this one was different. I had never before witnessed a preacher inviting all the teenagers to come to the altar and experience God's call on their lives. Although I wasn't sure exactly what that meant, I felt I had to step forward. Moved by faith, I joined many others that night. It was a special moment. I don't remember who prayed for me, I just know that I experienced God's holy presence filling my whole being, from head to toe. In that instant, I knew that I was no longer the same person.

At that camp, I realized that my dream of becoming a Computer Engineer was not necessarily God's dream for me. From that altar call, my enthusiasm for becoming a Computer Engineer began to wane. I wanted to give my life to serve Jesus. Although I wasn't sure what that looked like, I felt a burning passion for God within me. As the months went by, God began gave me little glimpses of what my future would be.

I thought he would be my husband

I remember one particular story when I decided to break up with my boyfriend. I was seventeen years old. I had met a great young man who was also called to the ministry. He had already given me a promise ring that I had accepted. I thought he would be my husband. I remember the day when, again, at an altar, God asked me to go to Bible College to prepare for the ministry. When I shared it with my boyfriend, he did not agree. He wanted us to marry as soon as I graduated from High School. He also shared with me a dream he believed God had given him. In that dream, he saw me in a wedding dress; he didn't see my face, but he saw my long hair from behind and was convinced it was me. He was a little confused. I was only seventeen years old, and I was at a crossroads in my life. Would I get married, or would I go to Bible College?

I learned that the Lord always reveals His will to you in a personal way. As I sought God, I was confident that He would speak to me. I firmly believed that He would guide me and reveal whether His will was for me to get married or to attend Bible College. Certainly, if God had spoken to my boyfriend through a dream, He would also speak to me. I prayed and prayed and prayed some more, taking time to seek God's direction. The more I prayed, the more conviction I felt that God was calling me to attend Bible College.

I will never forget that day. My boyfriend and I sat across from each other at the Steak House restaurant. I looked into his eyes, and with great conviction (and also sadness), I told him that I was absolutely certain that God was calling me to attend Bible College. With determination, I took off my promise ring and handed it to him. We blessed each other and went our separate ways.

I am thankful that God always finds a way to confirm to us that we made the right decision. In August 1990, I entered Bethany Bible College in Santa Cruz, CA. About nine months later, while I was in my dorm room, I received a call from one of my sisters. She informed me that she had seen an announcement in the newspaper about the engagement of my ex-boyfriend and his fiancé. I was a bit shocked. I asked her what she looked like. I had imagined that she would have long, brown, permed hair, just like my ex-boyfriend had seen in his dream. However, that was not the case. She turned out to be blonde and with straight hair. Immediately I felt the whisper of the Holy Spirit confirm that I had listened correctly to the Spirit of God and that I was in the right place at the right time. I was once again certain that God had a unique plan for my life.

If I could only be like her

During my first year in Bible College, I was looking for a new local church that I could call my spiritual home. I recall the day I set foot into Bethel Tabernacle Church in Watsonville, California. The building was unlike anything I had ever experienced. The seats were not traditional pews, but rather theater-type seating. I had arrived late, so I sat toward the back. That day they had invited a guest speaker. Her name was Erma Contreras. I will never forget her. She was a short woman, but very full of fire. When she preached, she used the whole platform. She spoke with power and authority. She completely captivated me during her sermon. I watched her as I thought to myself, "If only I could be like her!" My desire was to be used by God, but my natural personality was shy and reserved. I had never preached that way before, but I longed to do so.

The time came for Erma to minister at the altar. She began by praying for specific people. Then suddenly, she called out my name. She said, "Adelita, come here." I was shocked. I immediately thought that there must be another person in the service with the same name as me. But she looked directly at me and said, "You, Adelita, come here." I couldn't believe it! How did she know my name? I had never met her before. I stood up, knees trembling, and walked to the altar.

I never imagined that God would speak so powerfully. As soon as I got to the altar, Erma spoke with authority and told me, "God says never to desire to be like anyone else, but to long only to be who God has called you to be." No one had ever read my mind like that. How did she know what I was thinking? God was definitely speaking to me, and I knew He had a unique plan for my life. God's glorious presence was so tangible that I fell prostrate in the Spirit. After experiencing that intense presence of God, (the Shekinah glory), I got up again.

"God will be your provision"

God had more words of wisdom for me. Erma looked at me again and said, "God has something else to tell you." After my first experience, I knew I needed to pay close attention. Erma continued, "God knows you are worried about your finances and wondering how you are going to afford your education. But you don't need to worry; God will be your provider. Trust in Him." That word from

God was so accurate. I was really worried about my finances. My parents were unable to support me, and although I knew they would do everything they could to help me, I didn't want to put them in a difficult situation. That night I needed God's Word, and I was determined to believe it.

God is faithful to His Word. Throughout my education at Bethany College, I never ceased to be amazed at the blessings God showered upon me. I received anonymous offerings in the mail to cover my tuition. Every time I applied for a scholarship; it was granted. Semester after semester, I witnessed God's arm reach out to provide for me again and again. The total cost of my undergraduate education exceeded $60,000, and I only had to pay out of pocket $1,000. I never had to resort to student loans. God continued to demonstrate His faithfulness, as it is written in His Word: *'And my God will meet all your needs according to the riches of his glory in Christ Jesus'* (Philippians 4:19)

I became a licensed minister at twenty-one

I graduated from Bethany College in 1994. Those four years were truly transformational as my faith in Christ deepened, and my call continued to be confirmed. During that time, I had been serving in the Youth Ministry at Bethel Tabernacle for three years and had taken a 3-month mission trip to Cordoba and Buenos Aires, Argentina. Although I was still not completely clear on what God's next step was for me, I felt it was the right time to get my ministerial credential and continue to move forward in God's plan for my life. At the age of twenty-one, I was licensed as a minister by the Assemblies of God in the Southern Pacific District (formerly known as the Pacific Latin District).

Shortly after, new opportunities opened up through God's guidance. I was invited to work in the accounting offices of the Southern Pacific District in La Puente, CA., and also to serve as Pastor of Evangelism at one of our Assemblies of God churches. As a young minister, I watched godly men and women exercise their leadership gifts, and these places helped me grow. I am indebted to many outstanding ministers and parishioners who embraced me at this stage of my life as a young, single minister just starting on her journey.

Ministry is not always easy

Ministry is not always easy. It can be challenging. After five years of serving in my first official church as a licensed minister, the time for transition arrived. My transition was in the midst of much pain and, at times, confusion. It is hard for pastors or ministers to imagine leaving a church in a difficult situation. However, sometimes it happens, and God uses these situations to mold and form us. I thank God that four of the five years were exceptionally good, and I also thank God for the last year, which was very difficult and unexpected.

The difficult season began when my pastor's wife was in the last stage of cancer. It was very beautiful and meaningful the love, support, and backing that the church offered to our senior pastor and his wife. They were both reaping what they had sown for many years. However, the inevitable came, and our senior pastor's wife passed away and went to be with Jesus.

It is difficult for everyone to cope with the death of a loved one, and for a faith community, it is as well, also especially when it is one of the main leaders. Our church's experience was no different; it was layered with pain. Shortly after her death, the senior pastor decided to take a sabbatical and asked me to lead the church in his absence for several months. I loved the congregation and wanted to honor my pastor, so I accepted without hesitation. As a young minister, I gave my all. I preached, counseled, made hospital visits, comforted, loved, and served to the best of my ability. I was so grateful to God for His wisdom imparted to me in every situation. The text of James 1:5 tells us precisely about the wisdom we can ask God for with the certainty that we will receive it.

I learned at a young age that as ministers and disciples of Christ, we could give ourselves completely to Him, serve Him to the best of our ability, and yet problems can still arise. While I was doing my best to serve, I was accused of trying to take over the church. I was shocked and heartbroken to be framed in such a way. I was only twenty-six years old. I recognize that I made some mistakes due to my youth and inexperience, but I also knew that my only desire was to honor God and His church. However, two influential people within the congregation said harsh words against me, so the situation became even more painful. After receiving counsel from my spiritual leaders and much prayer, I realized it was time to make a transition. I cried. I was in deep pain. It hurt. It hurt a lot. I didn't want to leave that way. But I knew it was time to go. I knew God still had a plan for me, even though I couldn't see it clearly at that moment, and that He was faithful in both life's good and challenging seasons.

God's grace in my life

Reflecting on those years, I can clearly see God's hand of grace in my life. God can definitely take what the enemy (the devil) intended for harm and transform it into something good. Genesis 50:20 refers to this aspect. I can see how God allows us to go through difficulties for the purpose of growth. This personal experience has allowed the words of James 1:2-4 to become a reality in my life. Today I can affirm, just as James said, *"Consider it pure joy, my brothers and sisters, whenever you face trials of many kinds because you know that the testing of your faith produces perseverance. Let perseverance finish its work so that you may be mature and complete, not lacking anything."* No one wants to experience trials, but they produce great beauty if we go through them with Jesus.

What now, God?

God continued to shape my character. In January 2000, God led me to the magnificent Central Coast of California. I was invited to work with 'at-risk youth' in a para-church organization called City Impact in Oxnard. The first day of my new job was filled with excitement. I arrived early that first morning, but after a few hours, the President called me into her office to let me know that my position was no longer available. City Impact no longer had the financial resources to maintain my position. In that split second, my mind was filled with confusion. I had just relocated to a new city, leaving my church family, friends, and comfort behind, and now I was out of a job. I quickly asked myself, "Did I hear God wrong? Did I make a big mistake? What will become of my life now?"

God always knows what He is doing! I went to my new apartment that day. I lay prostrate on the floor, crying and asking God, "What now, God? Did I get it all wrong?" As I cried and questioned God about what I was experiencing, He began to instill peace in me. Little by little, I received more peace, and God reminded me of His presence, His provision, and His power in my life and that *He was the same yesterday, today, and forever,* as (Hebrews 13:8) says. As I pressed into His presence, I knew that I knew, that everything was going to be ok.

I obeyed!

During the following days, God gave me clarity about my next step in life. I was to continue preparing myself for service. God assured me that He would use my educational background to open doors to my future ministry. I obeyed. A few months later, I became a student at Fuller Theological Seminary in Pasadena, where I graduated with my Master of Divinity degree.

As a side note, a few weeks after I began my seminary studies, City Impact called to offer me the same position as before. I accepted. Once again, God allowed me to go through a challenging trial to mold my character and align me with His perfect will for my life. I encourage you to never fear in the face of a problem or difficult situation in your life. As children of God these storms make us more like Jesus and position us to fulfill God's plan for our lives. We may not like these storms at the particular time we go through them, but God uses these trials to prepare us to live the best life possible for the Kingdom of God. *Never doubt that God will work all things for the good of those who love him and have been called according to his purpose,* as it says in Romans 8:28.

And by the way, something incredible happened while I was at Fuller Theological Seminary. God continued to provide scholarships and offerings year after year, so I never needed to apply for a single loan. I remember driving home one night from seminary so thankful for God's provision. As I was driving, the Holy Spirit reminded me of the prophetic word God spoke to me in 1990 at Bethel Tabernacle Church through Erma Contreras. God had said I would never have to worry about His provision for my education. Even years later, God continued to fulfill His word. *Don't ever doubt that the Word of God never returns void. If He said it, He will accomplish it* (Isaiah 55:11).

Associate Pastor at Ventura First A/G

In 2002, God gave me the opportunity to join the Ventura First Assembly (VFA) pastoral team. I then became part of the SoCal Network (district). From the onset of my experience at VFA, I learned what it meant to have a male ally who would support and even fight for the leadership of a young, single Latina woman in ministry. Although our Assemblies of God denomination has ordained women for decades, the practice of women in pastoral positions (outside of youth and children) was not yet common. Therefore, it was not easy for some church members to accept my position as Associate Pastor.

I will forever be grateful to lead Pastor Tony Cervero for his willingness to take the hits and losses when some people left the church because of my intentional hiring to become a more diverse congregation. It was a challenging transition. Nevertheless, Pastor Tony was willing to pay the price to model the truth of Scripture that both men and women are equipped, gifted and equally called by God to build His kingdom. Galatians 3:26-28 says, "*For you are all sons of God through faith in Christ Jesus, for all who have been baptized into Christ have put on Christ. There is neither Jew nor Greek, slave nor free, male nor female, but all are one in Christ Jesus*" What a beautiful truth! As a young single Latina, I needed someone who believed in my calling and was willing to stand up for the truth of God's Word, and Pastor Cervero did!

Male pastors as allies make a difference

If you are a male lead senior pastor or associate pastor of a church, I encourage you to take on this same role and be an ally for a young woman or one who is just starting in ministry. Even today, we are still pioneering the way, and I can personally say that those male pastors, as allies, make a difference. I am convinced that men and women of all ages and ethnicities can build God's Kingdom more quickly and powerfully when they work together in partnership than when they work separately. And in doing so, we make the Kingdom about Jesus and not about ourselves.

God brought diversity to His church. It was beautiful to witness how a congregation, which was 97% Anglo, became a mix of different ethnicities, loving and serving one another. It took a lot of difficult conversations, losses, misunderstandings, and pain along the way, but the hard work was being done, and the church was becoming more and more like the Kingdom to which we will belong in heaven according to Revelation 5:9-10; 7:9-10.

We began a Spanish Ministry - (Ministerio Puente)

After three years at First Assembly of God in Ventura, in 2005, God began to stir in my spirit the possibility of starting a Spanish Ministry within First Assembly. Such a group would add another layer of diversity. After much prayer and conversation with the lead pastor, we decided to move forward and started Ministerio Puente. I had the privilege and responsibility of being the pastor of this new ministry. I continued as a part-time associate pastor, but I was also a part-time pastor of this new Spanish-speaking congregation.

It was a new and exciting journey for me. I had this unique opportunity to care for those who spoke only Spanish and develop a team to help care for this new congregation, Ministerio Puente. I must admit that for the next year, I felt a mixture of joy and sadness every day. There was so much to celebrate as people were saved and their lives were transformed. Yet, at the same time, I faced challenges similar to those I had faced at First Assembly of God, Ventura. As our Hispanic congregation began to grow, many of them had never experienced having a young, single Latina woman pastor. It was a different experience for many. There were a couple of men who, on various occasions, tried to discredit me and convince others that I was not called, qualified, or equipped to be a pastor. But God continued to provide spiritual authorities who protected and supported my pastoral calling. Personally, at this stage of my life, I was fully convinced that God had called and positioned me to be a pastor.

By the grace of God, Ministerio Puente continued to grow, and in one year, 2006, we were able to become financially self-sustaining, so I was hired as the full-time pastor of this ministry. After a few years, it became evident that God was leading us to transition from being a ministry within a church to becoming a church plant in another city. I began to pray along with the leadership of Ministerio Puente, as we knew that becoming a church plant meant taking on a new set of responsibilities that we had never experienced before.

God was calling me to be a church planter

God knew exactly how to convince me that I was to be a church planter. While we were praying for this purpose, Pastor Tony Cervero offered me a position as Executive Pastor at Ventura First Assembly. It was a sweet offer; the pay would be twice as much as I would receive if I chose to church plant. At the same time, I was accepted at Fuller Theological Seminary to begin a Ph.D. program. Sometimes I wasn't sure what to do, but I continued to lean on God to direct my path. Proverbs 3:5-6 was an inspiration to me in this regard.

As I continued to pray, God's voice became clearer and clearer, indicating to me that the executive pastor position was not for me, and that the additional salary would not satisfy me as much as complete obedience to Jesus. In addition, when I applied for scholarships for my doctoral program, I was not accepted, something I had never experienced before. God has always provided for my education. I remember sitting on my bed after being rejected regarding the scholarship, asking God, "Why aren't you providing?" I clearly remember hearing God's voice saying, "Because I am answering your prayers, you are going to establish a church instead of pursuing a Ph.D." At that moment, I was completely convinced about my next step in ministry. God was calling me to plant churches.

We established a new church in Santa Paula, CA

In 2010, God opened the doors to plant Puente de Vida Church in the city of Santa Paula. I have had the privilege of pastoring this wonderful church for thirteen years, It has been a beautiful journey, and I have served alongside incredible pastors and leaders. God has challenged me and led me in different directions, but through it all, the most enriching thing is personal and spiritual growth and, of course, God's faithfulness at all times.

Our vision from the beginning, is focused on improving the lives of people and their families with the love and transforming power of Jesus. To the honor and glory of our God, there are many people who have experienced salvation and transformation in Jesus Christ.

Every transition and every new step of faith has had its gains and losses, but I have learned that what is most important is our obedience to God. It is not always the easiest path, but it is always the most fulfilling and rewarding.

I remember that when we first launched Puente de Vida church, the facility we were going to rent closed its doors to us only two weeks before the launch.

It would have been easy to postpone the launch, but instead we prayed, and God gave us the possibility to start in the garage of an empty home. I questioned the location many times. It seemed ridiculous and had no appeal. Yet as we prayed, God told us, "Start in the garage of this house." So, we did! Our beginning was very humble. But God teaches us through Zechariah 4:10 that we should not despise humble beginnings.

97

Let me encourage you, dear reader. Never despise humble beginnings. Jesus' beginning was humble, for He was born in a manger, and look how He changed the world. We believe that our humble beginnings can change the world too!

We stayed in this garage for six months until the Santa Paula Assemblies of God church opened their doors to allow us to rent and share their building. For three years, we shared the building with the English congregation and then continued to rent the building on our own for nine years. During this time, although we were not the owners, we totally remodeled and cleaned the building.

A great blessing that could not be refused

Today we own our church facility. There are so many miraculous stories about how it happened, but I don't have enough space to share them all. I can briefly say that after twelve years of renting, caring for and investing in a facility that was not ours, God honored us in an amazing way. About nine months ago, I received a phone call from one of our Assemblies of God leaders offering to sell us the building. They mentioned how well we had managed the facility, and that they wanted to be a blessing to us. My ears were wide open to hear what that blessing would be, but I never imagined it would be so incredible. They offered us the opportunity to purchase the building, valued at $1.5 million for only $170,000. How could we turn down that blessing? Our answer was a resounding "YES!"

God always knows the moment when we need a miracle. I firmly believe that if we pray and faithfully obey our calling, God will always provide at the right time.

We started out as an only Spanish-speaking congregation and then became a bilingual congregation. Currently, we have both a Spanish-language congregation (Puente de Vida) and an English-language congregation (Bridge of Life). We also established a flourishing church in Puruándiro, Michoacán, Mexico, called Misión Puente.

We continue with a vision

For a couple of years, we prayed that God would provide us with a new location, as our current facility was getting small and lacked parking. We knew that in order to continue to grow, we needed another facility, but we did not have the financial resources to buy or build one. BUT GOD! He always knows, He always sees, and He is always in control. His power never runs out. We just have to keep believing in Him and trusting in His plan.

We must never stop dreaming and keep a vision alive in our hearts. If God has given that vision, He will provide the necessary resources to carry it out, according to His riches in glory. Today, we are fully confident that God will continue to provide for our relocation to a new building. Although we have not yet acquired the land and do not have all the financial resources, we recognize that there are several steps we must take in this process. However, we have many reasons to be confident: a faithful God who never abandons us, a vision from God Himself, a God who performs miracles, faith to move mountains, and the perseverance to keep believing until God opens the right door.

Your call comes from God

In closing, let me encourage you. Do not doubt your call whether you are single or married, a man or a woman, young or old, or whatever story or background you've experienced. Your calling comes from God, and no one can take that call from you. God has a special plan for you to fulfill. It is so unique and unlike any other. You are special, and God reminds you today that, as it says in Jeremiah 29:11 *"He knows the plans He has for you; they are plans to prosper you and not to harm you, plans to give you hope and a future."*

At the beginning and the end of every day, we all share the same purpose. And that is to glorify the Father and make Jesus famous throughout the whole world through the power of the Holy Spirit in us. Therefore, let us join together to exalt Jesus and bring as many souls as possible into the Kingdom of God. Together, let us move forward in this mission with perseverance and passion.

7. FAITHFUL TO THE LORD UNTIL THE END

Pastors Aldo & Liliana Suarez

Primera Asamblea de Dios, Victorville, CA

(Hispanic Ministries of First Assembly of God, Victorville, CA)

Liliana tells about her family

My earliest memories are of a small, humble house in a suburban neighborhood in Buenos Aires. My parents, Ana and Nicolas, had emigrated from Ukraine and Belorussia, respectively, in the 1930s, just before World War II.

My maternal grandmother, Maria, was the first to accept the Gospel message in her village through a Baptist missionary. She quickly opened her home for meetings. What a blessed time! With great emotion, my mother would tell me how she first heard about the baptism of the Holy Spirit and how she had that extraordinary experience alone, in the middle of the Odessa forests.

My father belonged to the communist party like most young students in his city, but he too heard the message of salvation, which changed the course of his life completely. From that moment on, he dedicated himself to the service of the Lord.

From Ukraine and Belarus to Paraguay to Argentina

The rumors and prophecies of an imminent war were intensifying, and many decided to leave the cold lands of that continent and emigrate to Paraguay, a country that opened its doors to many immigrants in those years. It was there that my parents met and married. Later they moved to Buenos Aires, Argentina, where I was born, the youngest of five siblings. My parents served the Lord together in the city's poorest neighborhoods, the so-called slums, known as the villas miseria back then. I can still remember the aromas of those corridors, with stagnant, dark water. The need was overwhelming in those places. The churches were few, and most were very small, which makes me think now about how much the Gospel has grown in Argentina, although there is still a lot to do.

My father was an outstanding expositor of the Word

My father, Don Nicolas, was an outstanding expositor of the Word of God, eloquent and very diplomatic. He traveled a lot carrying the Gospel message. His last trip was to his homeland after thirty-eight years, which was an exciting experience for him. Many brethren who had suffered war and persecution received him in a large hall, where he preached to them. It was a significant and special moment in his life. I keep with great affection a detailed letter he wrote about that trip, in which he recounted all the experiences he had lived. On his return, a few months later, he passed on to the presence of the Lord, having fulfilled his great desire.

My mother was a great servant of God

I was ten years old when my father passed away, and I remember that day very well. However, there was much to do. I had already accepted the Lord at a children's camp and understood clearly what it meant to serve God. It was time to continue in the work of the Lord and help my mom in whatever was needed. She was a great servant of God, I would have so many stories to tell about her! Her heart was focused on serving the poor and displaced. She cooked for them, sewed clothes for them, preached to them, and taught the women. Her life reflected the virtuous woman mentioned in Proverbs 31. Well, yes, that's what she was. She had no material ambitions; all her possessions fit into a small suitcase. And oh, how she interceded for her children! There are many stories I could tell of those times, but I will summarize by saying that our house was always a place where a church was established and that our neighbors were evangelized, thanks to her.

Immigrants to the USA

In 1979, we had to immigrate to the United States, where my older brother lived. The city of Seattle welcomed us with its characteristic rain and beautiful leafy pine trees. It was a new and great challenge, but we soon found a small church, Templo El Redentor, where we assembled and served.

Later, we moved to warm California, where we also met precious Christian brethren and congregations. During these years, we lived many experiences, some full of joy and others a little sad, but always thankful for God's faithfulness at every stage. In 1985, we had the opportunity to travel to Argentina to visit my sister-in-law and nieces, since my brother Miguel had passed away, and we had not been able to do it before.

It was a very emotional moment to see each other after six years and visit the church we had attended before immigrating to the United States.

Aldo continues with his story

I was born in a Christian home, the son of a Jewish mother and a father of Arab descent. Flora Zablotsky and Abdon Suarez.

Since I was a little boy, I always wanted to be a preacher like my father. When I was five years old, I used to climb a fig tree every Sunday. I would prepare my sound equipment, which consisted of a sardine can full of holes made with a nail and a hammer. That was my version of a microphone, and I would tie a string through one of the holes, connecting it to the speaker, which was a little yellow plastic bucket.

I would begin my Sunday service by singing a hymn from the hymnal. Then I would say to whoever would listen, "Christ is coming; repent of your sins!" And at the end, I would invite them to the evening meeting, where my dad was the pastor. I sang the chorus, "Christ is coming, there are signs, He is coming to look for saved souls. Those who sleep will stay, and those who watch will go with Him. I'm going with Him, going with Him, I'm not staying, I'm going with Him!"

One Sunday afternoon, Mr. Vicente Ruano came to church, saying that he had come because he listened every Sunday from his house to the child who shouted from the fig tree. That day he gave his life to the Lord.

"I will be faithful to the Lord until the end because I want to see you again"

I was nine years old when my dad went to be with the Lord. My dad's best friend, Enrique Aimo, gathered us together on the day of the wake and told my mom and my sisters, Blanca, Stella, and Alicia, "If you want to see your dad again, you have to be faithful to the Lord, until the end." So I went to the coffin, took my dad's hands, and told him, "I will be faithful to the Lord until the end because I want to see you again."

We were united in marriage on March 15, 1986

In my youth, I was actively serving as a youth leader, and in 1979, at a youth camp, I met Liliana. But she moved to the USA, and although I put my address in the Bible that we youth gave her, she never wrote to me.

In 1985, she returned with her mother for a visit to Argentina, and we met again. Although she had to return to the United States, we communicated by letter for five months. When she returned on October 13 of the same year, we continued our friendship, but already as fiancés. On December 24, 1985, I proposed to her, and we were married on March 15, 1986. The following year, we received with joy and expectation the news that we were expecting a baby.

It was a tremendously sad day

Our desire was to settle in the United States, so we made the necessary arrangements and obtained the visas. We traveled to Washington State, where Liliana's family was waiting for us. At that time, she was eight months pregnant. This part of the story is extremely painful because our baby died a few days before birth. It was a tremendously sad day. We only endured it with the help of the Holy Spirit. Although we were living and working in the midst of sadness, we remained hopeful.

God supplied all our needs

Two years later, we made the decision to attend the Bible Institute in La Puente, CA. A missionary friend helped us with transportation, and on January 15, 1990, we arrived at the Latin American Bible Institute with great expectations to learn. God was with us and supplied all our needs during our stay at the institute.

A beautiful couple from Alaska welcomed us with open arms and helped us find a place to live at the Bible Institute. This brother allowed me to work on the construction of the Hispanic Assemblies offices and the new dormitories for the students. This brother's wife got Liliana a job with the Christian organization World Vision. We worked with this couple in establishing a church and then were youth pastors at El Sendero de la Cruz church for two years. From there, we learned that a group of eighteen believers in Christ needed a pastor. So, I was asked if I was willing to put my hands to the plow. My wife and I replied, "Yes, of course!" We accepted the challenge without pay and carried out multiple occupations at the same time.

Our first church

Our first experience as pastors was at Echoes of Calvary Church. Initially, we rented the dining room of Rosemead Christian Center, an English-speaking Assemblies of God church in Rosemead, CA. However, within a few months of being there, the pastor of that church was elected to serve another congregation in California. At that time, the leaders of the SoCal Network (District) of the Assemblies of God offered us the opportunity to become the pastors of Rosemead Christian Center and transform it into a bilingual church.

When we accepted the position, we had to transfer our ministerial credentials from the Latin District to the geographic district, SoCal Network. Suddenly, we moved from the dining room to the main sanctuary and had our own building.

Against all odds, the church began to grow, even though we were in a predominantly Asian neighborhood. We were pastors in Rosemead for fifteen years.

Hispanic Ministries of the SoCal Network

I remember that at that time, our Hispanic Ministries Directors in the SoCal Network were missionaries, Wayne and Doris Turnbull. Also we were part of the formation and growth of the Hispanic Ministry that had been started by missionary Harry Bartel. Those were times of great fellowship, and soon after, missionaries Richard and Janice Larson took over the leadership of Hispanic Ministries. They are wonderful servants of God, with experience on the mission field and in the pastorate, and they became our mentors to whom we turned for advice on how to effectively carry out the ministry.

January 1996, Katelyn Mariel arrived

After the death of our first baby and the loss of two more pregnancies, in January 1996, our long-awaited Katelyn Mariel arrived in our marriage. She has served the Lord since she was a little girl and continues to do so as a worshiper.

"We want you to go and preach."

In the middle of 2006, Brother Larson, our Hispanic Ministries director, informed me that they were looking for a pastor for the Hispanic ministry in an English-speaking church in Victorville, CA. Previously, there had been a strong Hispanic ministry, but problems arose, and the leader, along with many brethren, had left. I remember saying to Brother Larson, "I will pray for the Lord to send a pastor." He replied, "We want you to go and preach." At that time, I was comfortable with my current situation, being bi-vocational; I could attend to various tasks, with the flexibility to do work outside the church and manage my own schedule.

At a certain point, I had mentioned to Pastor Larson that if a need arose in a Hispanic ministry in an English-speaking church, I would like to have that experience. And now, that need was presenting itself.

So, on Sunday, October 15, 2006, my wife and I went to the high desert to Victorville to preach, and the brethren began to say, "¡We now have Argentine pastors!" However, we had not yet made any decision. I asked the Lord if we should accept that challenge, and we took it to prayer.

After speaking with the senior pastor, I realized that my starting salary would be less than what I had been earning. However, the Lord showed me in Philippians chapter 2, that He had left His comfort zone to serve where there was a need. So I thought, "If I want to be an imitator of Christ, I must follow in His footsteps.

Let's say yes, and in due time, He will honor us." And so, it happened.

The Hispanic Ministry began to grow

In December 2006, we assumed the role of pastors of La Primera Asamblea de Dios, the Hispanic ministry of First Assembly of God in Victorville, CA. In two years, without doing evangelistic work, we experienced growth from thirty to one hundred and eighty, and over the years, we reached an attendance of five hundred and fifty people in our two Sunday services.

These were years of victory, joy, and hard work. During this time, we witnessed hundreds of people give their lives to Christ. In addition, we invested time and energy to train many workers. With the support of our senior pastor John Martin and the exceptional brethren who responded affirmatively to the eternal call, we were able to establish three Hispanic ministries on our Victorville First Assembly campuses.

The following leaders are already in charge of their respective Hispanic ministries; Pastors Pablo and Alejandra Gamino in Apple Valley, CA; Pastors Salvador and Blanca Flores in Hesperia, CA; and Pastors Joel and Lilian Elizondo, Lucerne Valley, CA.

We left the church in July 2019 to begin our journey toward our missionary calling.

Our deepest thanks to all of you

The El Sendero de la Cruz Church, Echoes of Calvary, and Rosemead Christian Center gave me the opportunity to grow in ministry, continue my Bachelor of Theology studies at Latin American Theological Seminary, as well as obtain my Master's degree at Azusa Pacific University.

Liliana earned her B.A. in Christian Counseling, and later I earned my Doctorate in Ministry from the International Bible College and Seminary. We are infinitely grateful for the patience they have had during our growth and formation as pastors.

We thank the Primera Asamblea de Dios of Victorville and the incredible team of pastors who believed in us and gave us the opportunity to serve. We also want to thank the brethren from the seventeen nations represented in our church, who taught us to love and respect their culture, and from whom we reaped many friendships. We carry you continually in our hearts and pray for abundant blessings in your lives and ministries. To all of you, thank you! Only eternity will reveal the impact that each of you has made and continues to make with your faithfulness to the Lord and His work.

I bless the Lord for the pastors who succeeded us, who have taken the church from blessing to blessing. And, of course, I thank the district leaders who were always present to support us.

We are now missionaries

Today we are facing a new challenge, almost in the twilight of our lives. We are missionaries with the Assemblies of God World Missions – AGWM.

God called us to return to Argentina. We are striving to fulfill the desire of Jesus, to take the Gospel first to the Jew and also to the Gentiles. Romans 10:1 says, "*Brethren, my heart's desire and prayer to God for Israel is for salvation.*" (RV 1960)

Our assignment is to raise awareness in the church about the importance of taking the message of the Messiah to the Jewish people. We ask you to pray for us! Once again, we have answered "Yes!" to God. We are ready to put our hands to the plow once again.

8. SADNESS WAS TURNED INTO JOY

Pastors José & Silvia Barrios

Iglesia Roca Firme, Bellflower, CA

(Written with the help of their son José Barrios, Jr., who was part of the congregation and of this story)

José Q. Barrios was born in Durango, Mexico, where he led a chaotic life full of sin because he did not know God. His companions or friends called him "la pólvora" (the gunpowder) because he was quick to ignite and come to blows with his adversaries. He and his friends committed misdeeds, drunkenness, and so on.

However, he always worked with his father, delivering beer to the ranches. He also had many other jobs.

He heard about God for the first time

The first time José heard about God was in a town where they took him and other schoolmates to perform a drama where he played Pancho Villa; They stayed in different houses, and he was placed in a Christian home. Before eating, they prayed for the food, and at the end of his stay, they gave him a small bible as a gift.

He came to this country (USA) and met his wife

José was very young when he came to this country (USA) and worked various jobs while continuing his drunken binges. One day when working in a winery, he met Maria Campana, who came from Santa Barbara to work at the same winery. She attended a church in Santa Barbara, where they were holding an evangelistic campaign; she invited José to the campaign, and he and his two brothers attended. It was there that he met his wife, Silvia.

José accepted Christ and left behind his addiction

José was driving down the highway from Tijuana when he experienced a turning point in his life. While driving under the influence of alcohol, he was stopped and taken to jail. There, he had a profound conversation with Christ and said, "Help me if you are real. I accept you as my Savior, and I will never drink beer again." Since that day, José has kept his promise and has never tasted beer again. His encounter with Christ marked the beginning of a new life away from his addictions.

When José gave his life to Christ, he was transformed into a powerful force for the glory of the Lord. That individual who was once impulsive and used by the enemy in Durango was a new person. Since José came to know Christ, he immersed himself in constant Bible reading and shared his faith with all those he met, desiring for them to experience what he had found in God. He became a fervent evangelist and witness to the grace and love of

Christ. When José gave his life to Christ, that gunpowder the enemy had used in Durango at will, God turned it into dynamite for Christ.

One day while working as a driver in a fruit and vegetable market, a co-worker approached him and said, "José, listen, you are always so happy, singing, and joyful; tell me what you are using?" José replied, "Okay, I'll see you on the way out; I'll wait for you in my truck." And when he left, the young man rubbed his hands together, anxious to receive what would be shared with him. When he got into the truck, he was surprised because José was reading the Bible, and the young man said, "Oh, is that it?" He thought they would give him some drugs or something like that. And there, José shared with him the word of God. From that moment on, the life of that young man and his family were transformed, and now they all serve God.

Our family started going to a church in El Monte, CA, where they gave José a Sunday school class to teach. He sang in the choir, evangelized on Saturdays, and visited the church members who had missed the church services. He also picked up people to take them to church when they had no transportation.

The birth of the Roca Firme Church in 1998

The Sunday school classes that José was in charge of were taught to a small group of approximately fifteen Spanish-speaking people. One day, the pastor asked José if he would accept the challenge of pastoring those people, to which he immediately responded that he agreed. That is how Roca Firme Church was born, and José began his work as a pastor.

José, full of fervor and dedication, visited the sick both in hospitals and in their own homes, being a source of encouragement and comfort to them. He always carried with him a bag of food to share. It did not matter to him that he did not receive a salary from the church, as his livelihood came from the vegetable market he owned. From the beginning, José understood the importance of giving his tithes and did so with joy and gratitude.

In 1999, José received his first ministerial credential with the Southern California Assemblies of God.

Fire on the roof of the church

José gave counseling to brothers and sisters who had problems in their marriages. Once a month, he would hold prayer vigils from 6:00 p.m. until 6:00 a.m. the next day. As a community, they also gathered every morning at 5 a.m. for a time of prayer.

One day the pastor of the English-speaking church told José that the Police had come to the church after receiving a call that someone had seen fire on the roof of the church. When the policemen came in, they saw everyone kneeling and praying. When they saw that everything was in order, they left, and those who were praying did not even realize that the police had visited them.

They opened other works

José started a work in Mexico where they brought food and also shared the word of God. Someone went there every week. He also opened another work in Santa Fe, where there is a large church where people come from different parts of the country to work in the fields. They have taken the gospel to their places of origin, and some even pastor there.

Jealousy set in, and it was very painful

Pastor José, along with us the family, pastored the Roca Firme Church for several years, sharing the building with the English church, when unfortunately, jealousy arose in the mother church.

One day, without warning, the pastor of the English-speaking church said to José, "We want to make changes, and it's your turn to be part of the change. Next Sunday, you must say goodbye to your congregation. It will be best if you do not talk to anyone, and you will only tell them what is written on this paper."

To avoid being questioned by the brethren in the church and having to talk to them about the matter, José decided to leave and spend the week in Santa Fe, where he had planted a new church.

114

Despite everything, the Pastor did have mercy on Pastor Jose by not telling him sooner because his mother had recently died, and perhaps they wanted to spare him one more pain.

He told them what was written on the paper

Pastor José returned to be present on that Sunday when he was to say goodbye to the congregation, and so he did. He only told them what was written on the paper he had been given.

When José finished, he grabbed his Bible and headed for the exit. The brethren shouted to José, "We want to know why you have to leave the church!" All the brethren began to get up and follow José, like little sheep following their shepherd. Some were even crying. In the parking lot, they decided to meet in a nearby park to hold their service. There they agreed that each family would contribute $1000 to buy a church building.

A new temporary location for the church

The following Sunday, they did not have to meet in the park because a church brother, who maintained the garden at a church in Norwalk, told the pastor what had happened, and he gave them shelter. For the first two months, he didn't even charge them rent. After that, they paid rent and were there for two years.

The congregation continued saving money to buy a church building, and finally, the day came. They started looking at places, such as shopping malls, closed banks, and a piece of land that belonged to the Catholics. However, Pastor José didn't like any of them, but he was confident that God had something better for them.

They found a building for the church!

The entire congregation searched until they found the building where they are now. It was an Adventist church in Bellflower, CA, beautiful, with all the amenities, and well-equipped.

The asking price was $400,000, but the entire church had only been able to raise $40,000. The seller decided to lend them $20,000, but a down payment of about $100,000 was required. The Assemblies of God agreed to refinance the remaining $300,000.

José takes a step of faith

A considerable amount of money was still needed when Pastor José had the brilliant idea to refinance his house. Pastor Jose and Silvia did just that, and in this way, the necessary money was completed. The building was purchased, and the congregation celebrated the first service in their new building on New Year's Day, 2000. God had everything under control, as many more people have come to know the gospel in this new place.

Pastor José continued studying and preparing himself, and in 2013 he received his Ordination Ministerial credential. After twenty-five years, José and Silvia Barrios continue pastoring their precious Roca Firme Church.

"THUS, OUR SADNESS WAS TURNED INTO JOY!"

9. A CHURCH THAT CHANGES LIVES

Pastors Ramon & Mariela Camacho

First Assembly of God and Primera Asamblea de Dios, Huntington Park, CA

It is truly inspiring when we look back and see all that God has done. In the midst of the rush and busyness of everyday life, we often don't take the time to pause in our journey and recognize how many times we have witnessed God's power.

Mariela: Product of a mighty miracle

Our story begins in two countries far from each other. I was born in San Juan, Argentina, and Ramon in Guadalajara, Mexico. Both facing challenging situations. In my case, for me, it was the result of a powerful miracle.

My parents were facing a marital crisis. My father did not want to have any more children, to the point of forcing my mother to have a clandestine abortion, to which she agreed out of fear. She was never a victim of physical violence, but she was the victim of emotional violence, which is equally harmful. During the abortion procedure, my mother prayed and asked God to save that baby's life. Although she had not given her life to Jesus, she knew God was real and could perform miracles.

Supposedly the abortion procedure was successful, but as the months passed, my mother's womb began to grow and grow, and I was born in late 1973. It all seemed like a great mystery, even to the registered nurse, one of my closest aunts, who performed the abortion. No one understood what had happened.

Approximately forty years later, during a hysterectomy performed on my mother, her doctor was shocked and said, "Ma'am, did you know you have two uteruses?" She was amazed to see how great our God is. The doctor explained to her that this happens in one in a thousand cases. Without a doubt, they had performed the abortion in the empty uterus. Psalm 139 describes my story, for everything the Heavenly Father created in me was written in His book, with nothing missing.

My parents met Jesus eleven years after my birth, and in Him, everything became new. I must emphasize that my relationship with them is excellent, and there is no resentment. I can only say how merciful and great is our God.

Ramon: The call to the priesthood seemed to be my only destiny

My story begins differently. I was born into a very devout Roman Catholic home in Guadalajara, Jalisco, Mexico. From a very early age, I felt a strong urge to serve God, and the only way I saw to do so was to become a priest. At the age of eleven, I was impressed by the life of the Franciscan monks and decided to talk to the local parish priest about it. However, I was deeply disappointed when they explained that since my parents were not married in the Catholic Church when I was born, I was not eligible for the seminary or the monastery. I now understand that God, in His immense love, was already at work in my life without my knowing or understanding it.

My classmates invite me to their church

It wasn't until I turned twenty-one and immigrated to the United States, attending night classes to learn English, that some of my classmates invited me to a special event at their church. I accepted their invitation with some reluctance, more out of courtesy to them since it was not a Catholic church.

Upon entering that church in the city of Costa Mesa, CA, I immediately perceived a sweet, light, almost captivating atmosphere. As the praise music played, I watched the people worship with joy and reverence. When the time came, the preacher stepped up to the pulpit. His Brazilian accent in Spanish was remarkable. As he told the story of God's love in dying for my soul and my sins on the cross, he began to describe what a life without Christ was like and its eternal destiny.

In spite of considering myself a good person, without vices and trying to respect everyone without getting into trouble, during the whole time the evangelist was speaking, I felt that he was addressing me directly. So, when he made the call to give my life to Jesus, something inexplicable, almost magnetic, happened. I raised my hand, and with tears streaming down my face, walked from the back row to the front, while a warm, sweet certainty of immense divine

119

love flooded my whole being. At that moment, the vocation to serve God took on a deeper meaning than ever before. I began by helping the ushers, teaching the children, then participated in a discipleship group, and finally became involved with the youth group.

My pastor, Ramon Coronado, made the decision to open an extension of the Latin American Bible Institute, LABI. With an inexplicable clarity of God's call, but not knowing exactly where or how, I began to take classes in theological and ministerial instruction.

"He calls you to serve Him among the nations"

One day, one of the young men from the church invited me to accompany him to downtown Santa Ana. It was a Saturday morning, and in the midst of pleasant spring weather, the streets were full of passersby and merchants, the vast majority being of Mexican origin.

Suddenly, a group of about a dozen people of distinctly Asian origin emerged, walking with determination. One of them jumped up on a public bench and began preaching in Spanish about the love of Christ. He recited short phrases he had clearly memorized, shouting, "Christ loves you and died on the cross for you!" which his entire group repeated loudly. I was petrified and moved, not understanding how a group of Koreans were talking about God to my people. I waited patiently, but most people ignored them or laughed at them. Only a few of us listened attentively.

When they seemed to have finished, I approached the leader and asked him in English if there were any legal limitations to preaching on the streets, for I wanted to do it too. While that man was telling me that he was the pastor and that he had not been censored up to that point, a small, petite old woman from his group knelt down next to us, putting her face in the concrete of the sidewalk, thinking that her pastor was evangelizing me. Seeing that people were almost stepping on her, indifferent to her presence, I asked the pastor to tell her to get up, as I was already a Christian.

When he spoke to her in Korean, that woman stood up and looked at me with the most tender gaze I have ever seen and said something in her native tongue. I asked the pastor to please translate what she had said, to which he replied, "The Lord knows you have doubts, but He calls you to serve Him among the nations." Those words pierced my whole being, and I was moved to tears. That day, Jesus once again confirmed His call on my life through His sweet and faithful servant.

God always provided

So I immediately talked to my pastor, and with the savings I had, I went to study full-time at LABI in La Puente, California. Although those savings were only enough for the first semester, God always provided job opportunities to pay for my studies at the institute without dropping out of school.

One of the many anecdotes about divine provision during my preparation for God's calling occurred when I needed five dollars' worth of gas to travel to my church, La Puerta Abierta, in Costa Mesa. There was always some chore to be done, such as mowing a neighbor's lawn or washing a Bible school teacher's car, which allowed me to get exactly that five dollars needed for the round trip. However, on one particular weekend, none of that happened. Despite asking people, no one seemed to need my help. So, prayerfully I said, "Lord since you have not provided, I will stay for the school chapel service."

However, early that Sunday, I decided to go out to exercise in the nearby park. When I returned, I noticed that due to the rain the night before, water was running down the sidewalk ditches, washing away the trash. And suddenly, I could hardly believe it: there floating in the rainwater was a five-dollar bill! It was not a one-dollar bill, not a ten-dollar bill, but exactly a five-dollar bill. God was always faithful in similar ways; sometimes, to eat, I only had peaches from the trees at school, but that too is the work of God's hand.

Mariela: God always surprises us

It was at the age of eleven when I gave my heart to Jesus. I began serving God at the age of thirteen as a leader in a children's church, where every week, we gathered around eighty little ones who learned about God and His word. Surprisingly, many of them were my age. I understand that when God calls you, He also empowers you. At fifteen, I was called to be part of a youth leadership committee, which was a time of great learning and gratification. At twenty-one, I was ordained as a preacher in Argentina and had the opportunity to participate in several mission trips and church planting in rural areas.

Everything seemed to be fine, and I felt complete, thinking that this place would be the place where I would serve the Lord. However, God always surprises us, and after graduating from my Bible studies in my country, I began to feel a burden in my heart for missions. After talking with my pastor, he sent me to a group of people with a missionary calling who met weekly for prayer and planning. Each of us in that group was sent to different places, such as Nepal, England, Africa, and Europe. My question to the Lord was, "Where would you send me?"

My heart began to beat strongly for the United States of America. I thought that perhaps God had made a mistake since this nation was the cradle of missionaries, going all over the world. Nevertheless, in obedience, I decided to take that step of faith. I arrived in the United States on September 8, 1997, with little money in my pocket, but with a firm call to service, and determination to advance in my theological studies and thus fulfill God's purpose in my life.

I have to emphasize that the Lord used many people to bless my life during my time of preparation at the Latin American Bible Institute in La Puente, California. How can I not mention Simon Melendres, Irene Trinidad, the Acentares and Goleviosky family, Denis Rivera, Victor Mendez, Sister Keyri, and so many others who made a difference in my calling. I always had a roof over my head, food on the table, clothes and shoes, and even some small luxuries. When God sends us, and we are obedient to His voice, He always provides for our needs.

We were God's best for each other

That wonderful place gave me the opportunity to meet my life partner in this incredible adventure of fulfilling our eternal purposes together. During our theological preparation process and in a casual conversation, we discovered that our calling was exactly the same. Not only that, but it seemed like we had known each other forever. Finally, we found each other, something neither of us had planned for, but it happens, not at the time we desire, but at the time God has destined for our lives to be forever joined to someone.

Although the decision will always be ours, in my case, twenty-five years after that encounter, I can say with certainty that God did not make a mistake in bringing us together. We were God's greatest gift to each other. Our courtship lasted seven months, and four months after graduating from school, we were married. Although our original plan was to work, save and secure financial stability before taking that step, divine intervention was truly miraculous. God, as the owner of the gold and silver, became our Father provider.

God opened unexpected doors for us

After ministering in a mission where we served every Sunday, we were invited to lunch by a humble but generous-hearted couple. During the meal, questions came up about our marital situation, and upon mentioning that we were beginning to save for our wedding, the man named Martin replied with a smile, "But that's very simple, you just go to the bank and withdraw what you need." Inside we laughed because we had just opened a savings account, which was very meager. It was then that Martin and his wife Oralia surprised us by saying, "God has spoken to us and led us to cover your wedding expenses." They explained to us that over the years, they had accumulated wealth due to Martin's hard work in the fields of California, and then over the years, he started a business that prospered through his faithfulness to God, and now he was selling his product to markets as large as Walmart.

We didn't want to accept it at first, but they urged us that we should learn to receive God's blessings. It was a great lesson for both of us. We realized that God is omniscient, and interestingly, a week before, the Lord instructed us to look up the prices of everything we would need for our wedding.

The wedding was on, but we wondered where we were going to live. Once again, God worked a miracle through Pastor Ray Mesa, who was in charge of the Bible school apartments. He approached Ramon and said, "God has laid a burden for you on my heart. Is everything all right?" Ramon told him everything was fine and told him he was getting married and was looking for a place to live. Pastor Mesa then told him, "An apartment just vacated, and I feel you are the one I should give it to." Normally, there was a long waiting list for an apartment, but the person who was originally going to get it changed his plans and offered his place. No doubt God was opening unexpected doors for us.

God has demonstrated His faithfulness in the care of each of our three children

Our wedding was a marvelous experience in which we felt deeply blessed by our Heavenly Father. Just one year into our marriage, our firstborn son, David, was born. Labor had to be induced at eight months gestation due to a complication during pregnancy. While we waited for the medication to speed up the delivery, the unborn baby had a probe inserted into the skin of his little head. During a critical moment when Mariela's blood pressure increased dramatically, and the monitor displaying our little one's heartbeat stopped completely, as a first-time parent, I desperately cried out to the Heavenly Father. In answer to my fervent prayer, my son's newly formed heart began to pound almost instantaneously. It was a palpable miracle.

After our second anniversary, Paloma came into our lives, followed by Daniel precisely one year later. Each of our children brought a unique joy to our family. As the Lord formed our family, we felt an inexplicable certainty that He would care for us and our children each step of the way.

Over the years, we have undoubtedly witnessed God's care in our children's lives. At the age of three, Paloma experienced spontaneous healing from a severe case of allergy to grass, pollen, and almost any plant, which caused asthma attacks and aggressive skin rashes. At the age of eight, Daniel was diagnosed with Pectus Carinatum, a malformation in his chest cavity, and Marfan Syndrome, which affects his connective tissue. However, prayer, both ours and that of many other believers, was used by God to glorify and surprise us and the doctors. Although they did not understand how, the doctors affirmed that none of our children would suffer repercussions in time. Truly, we serve a sweet and merciful Christ who heals.

Upon graduating from high school, David enlisted in the Marine Corps, where he served as a reservist until he received a medical discharge due to an eardrum injury during gunnery practice. Paloma also joined the Army as a reservist.

God has demonstrated His faithfulness in caring for each of our three children at every stage of their lives up to the present. However, the most recent display of His protection was in the year 2021. As David waited for the green light at an intersection traffic light, his vehicle was struck by a young motorcyclist who was fleeing at high speed from the highway patrol. The collision was so violent that it completely wrecked the front of our son's medium-sized vehicle. The impact was on the passenger side, and when several officers arrived at the accident scene, they informed us that if the crash had occurred just sixteen inches further back, David would have suffered the same tragic fate as the young motorcyclist, who was killed instantly. However, David left completely unscathed, with only two minor scratches. I will never cease to thank God for His protective hand at that crucial moment.

The process of finding a church began

But going back to when we first graduated from Bible College, we wondered where God wanted us to be at that time. Through a chance meeting with the superintendent of the Southern California District of the Assemblies of God, Pastor Ray Rachels, and thanks to the recommendation of our dear mentors, missionaries Floyd, and Millie Woodworth, we had the opportunity to have an interview with the Director of Hispanic Ministries, our beloved Brother Richard Larson. Thus began our process of searching for the church where we would serve and fulfill our mission.

We received a call introducing us to Brother Fred Cottriel, former superintendent of the Southern California District. Soon we visited a church that was on the verge of closing. However, it was a great blessing to discover that they had their own building. From the moment we learned about the Huntington Park First Assembly of God in California and walked its streets, we realized the tremendous need that existed in that area of Los Angeles County.

January 2000, we began as pastors of First Assembly of God, Huntington Park, CA

The church had experienced a significant decline; services were conducted in English, and there were only four elderly people and a small group of eight young people. However, we fell in love with the place and, more importantly, the challenge it presented. Unfortunately, the building was not properly maintained, and there was much to be done. Curiously, we even encountered cockroaches and mice, which on one occasion, participated in the service, sticking their heads out from behind a piece of furniture.

So it was that in January 2000, we began as pastors of that church, aware of its great needs but also of the potential it had to make a difference. But just one month after we started, one of the eight young people, who was facing psychiatric problems, decided to take his own life in one of the church's classrooms. It was one of the most painful and saddest episodes we have ever experienced. We felt powerless to do anything about it, and as a result of this

126

traumatic situation, the small group of young people dispersed. In spite of everything, we decided not to give up, but to honor the memory of this young man by working to prevent others from going through what he had gone through. Sadly, one of the elderly women moved out of town, and another passed away.

In the midst of this process, as we continued to provide services in English, we began to notice the demographic changes in our community. It was then that we made the decision to start bilingual services. The church began to grow, but it would not be until God opened the doors to a 30-minute weekly Monday slot on a local television channel that the program "Voice of Hope" would begin. From that moment on, the church experienced significant growth, and we had the opportunity to meet many people who found their spiritual home in our church.

The miracle we needed for our Hispanic Church

At that time, the Huntington Park church underwent a transformation and became a Spanish-speaking church, while the youth and children continued to receive instruction in English. As time progressed, several challenges arose, one of the main ones being the lack of space. The place became too small to accommodate all the children and youth who came with their parents. Faced with this problem, we began to pray for more space.

In an act of faith and without fully understanding why, Ramon decided to write a letter to the lawyers of a firm that operated next to the church and who owned their property in partnership.

Years later, we received a letter from the senior partner inquiring if we were interested in buying their property, as they were planning to retire. To our surprise, we discovered that this man was a brother in Christ and informed us that although they had received other offers, they wanted to give priority to the church. At that moment, we realized that our God had already performed half of the miracle we needed.

Faith without works is dead

At that time, the country was going through a period of economic recession, but we knew that God is the owner of all things, and we decided to act in faith. We started knocking on doors, understanding that faith without works is dead. As we prayed and knocked on those doors, God used our beloved Brother Fred Cottriel to guide us in the process of purchasing that much-needed space for our church.

However, Pastor Fred passed into the presence of the Lord the same day the purchase process was closed. We want to emphasize that he was able to see with the eyes of faith those children and young people running in those new classrooms, filling themselves with the presence of Christ. It was a privilege to have met him, and we are grateful for the special way God used him in our story.

During the following years, the church experienced a process of consolidation, forming leaders and sending some of them to the School of Ministry. In addition, many people passed through our church, being impacted by God's love. In the Los Angeles area, it is common for people to move to places with a lower cost of living and greater job opportunities over time. God allowed us to be a link to make a difference in their lives and to then be sent by God.

A church that changes lives

If we had to define Huntington Park Church, we would dare to say that it is a transforming church. Over the years, we have witnessed countless supernatural miracles, doors opening in inexplicable ways that, without divine intervention, would never have opened. We have witnessed people trapped in chains being set free in a powerful way.

It is also important and healthy to recognize those things that meant sacrifice for us as ministers of the gospel. One of those challenges was facing the slow migration process in this nation, which prevented us from sharing with our family in our home countries.

Despite this difficulty, we were able to see God's faithfulness in the midst of this journey and process. He guided and strengthened us, and we finally saw the light at the end of the tunnel. We understood that God was calling us to be in this place and that we had to be faithful to His call.

10. THE CHURCH FULFILLING ITS MISSION

Pastors Heber & Betty Paredes

Iglesia La Puerta Abierta, Irvine, CA

I remember it was during a missionary service when my wife and I received the call from God to dedicate ourselves to the ministry. We were both fully involved in the activities of our church, my wife oversaw the children's ministry, and I was a member of the Official Body or board of directors of the church. We were both well established in our secular jobs; my wife worked in accounting for a bank in Guatemala City, and I worked as a professor in the Faculty of Architecture at the National University. I also had a professional office where I developed architectural design and construction projects.

The call to the ministry involved challenges for us, so we began to pray and prepare ourselves because the call was to dedicate ourselves to full-time ministry. Our three children were of school age, so if we stayed in Guatemala City, there would be no problem. However, I felt a deep need to prepare myself in the Word of God, and the best options for a solid preparation in the Word were outside the country.

Heber: My parents were pastors

It was relatively easy for me to adapt to the demands of the call to ministry. I was born and raised with my parents being pastors. I knew, albeit second-hand, some of the sacrifices and demands of the pastor's life and had had the excellent example of dedication and ministerial zeal instilled in me by my parents.

Although it is not easy to be the son of a pastor, our environment, social relationships, and world began and ended in the church. As a child, one absorbs the Christian life and relationships with the brethren in a normal way. However, when one reaches adolescence, the questions start to surface, the whys and wherefores, and of course, the temptations. Like any teenager, I began to question everything.

As a pastor's son and a member of a large family, I experienced the limitations of life economically austere. There were nine of us, six boys and three girls, and I was the second to last.

"Get up and go buy groceries for the pastor's family"

Although we had limitations, we never lacked food, God provided what was necessary for the daily feeding of nine people, and sometimes He did it miraculously. I remember one occasion when the children were in school, and the older ones were working; we returned home at noon to eat. In Guatemala, the midday meal, "el almuerzo" (lunch), has always been the most important meal of

132

the day; even after the single workday was established and most workers began to eat at or near their workplaces.

My mother was at home and had no provisions. There was no food for her children, who would come at noon. She, like my father, was a woman of prayer. It was about nine in the morning, and she was praying, crying out to God for the provisions of that day. At about eleven in the morning, there was a knock on the door. My mother went to open it; a sister from the church had come with a large basket loaded with groceries.

She told my mother, "Sister Isabel, I was praying a while ago in my house, and God spoke and told me, 'Get up and go buy groceries for the pastor's family and take them right now.' That is why I am here." Because of experiences like this, God has given me faith and gratitude to serve Him with all my heart. Reading a Bible verse with a promise from God is not the same as having experienced His reality in my own life. *I was young, and am old, and have not seen the righteous forsaken, nor his seed begging bread (Psalm 37:25).*

My first pair of shoes was at age eight

I went barefoot during my first seven years of life. My parents had enough money for clothes but not for shoes. However, my mother, who always tried to help my father economically, was always looking for money to buy me shoes. She owned a "Singer" (brand) sewing machine, and I still remember how she sewed new clothes on that machine for us and clothes from time to time for neighbors or siblings who asked her to do so. That's how she scraped together enough money to buy my first pair of shoes when I was eight years old. I can't forget the laughter of the neighbor kids when they saw me with those tremendously big black boots, like the ones used by soldiers, after seeing me barefoot all my life.

Whenever I read Proverbs 31, two women especially come to my mind, my mother and my wife. They have been, for me, like seeing an updated portrait of the virtuous woman.

133

The times of rebelliousness arrive

With everything and the excellent example of my parents, the times of rebellion arrived, of wanting to experience what the world has to offer; thank God, I never fell into vices, nor did I stray completely from the path; I did stray from communion and faithfulness to the church. However, I can sincerely say that I never lost or departed from the fear of God. There is no doubt that my parents' prayers did not allow me to stray completely. I remember that when my mother realized that the older children were not walking closely with God, she would go to the bed of each of them, kneeling with her arms on their pillows, she would cry out to God, saying, "Lord, my children belong to you. The devil has enough children, but mine are yours." Of the nine children, eight are or were in the ministry. The only woman not full-time in ministry served the Lord with all her heart, and three of her children are full-time pastors.

My father would gather us at the table daily at breakfast and dinner to pray, read the Bible, and instruct us based on the Word of God. It was daily devotional life. My wife says that even though she was not a Christian, she was eager to hear about the things of God; although she had studied in a Catholic school, they never talked to her about God.

An interesting thing to mention is that while I was somewhat apart from fellowship in the church, I met the one who is now my wife. However, according to her, it was what I talked about that attracted her the most to me. When we met, I spoke to her about the things of God; I was not in full communion, but I had no other conversation topic but what I had lived and received since childhood.

My life centered around the Christian faith and harmony with God, so that was my best topic of conversation.

My wife's childhood was relatively happy

Betty, my beloved wife, was born into a traditionally Catholic home, but like most, they only went to church on special occasions. However, she enjoyed a relatively happy childhood, which she spent living in a large house where there were several cousins with whom they played and had fun every day.

When they left that house, it was because her father could buy a place of his own, so she grew up in a family with certain economic solvency. She was the eldest of three siblings, her brother, who followed her, and her younger sister. They all attended private schools, and while her brother studied at the Polytechnic School, our country's military school, she and her sister entered the university to pursue their higher studies.

Their parents used to take them on trips to various places in our country, mainly to the house of her maternal grandparents, where she has many memories. However, when the local young people began to show interest in her and brought her many gifts, my father-in-law decided to stop visiting that place. God bless him for that decision!

Betty lived in New York City for a year

My father-in-law had a customs agency, and for some reason, when I was about 20 years old, I started working in that agency; by then, my wife-to-be was in the United States, where her father had sent her after finishing her studies. She lived in New York City for one year, where she had unique experiences. Being young and single, she initially lived with her uncle, but because he was involved in the drug business, she had to find another place to live.

She says that during that year, she saw things she had never known or seen in her life. Such as riding alone on the New York subway, advances and provocations at work, a cousin who wanted to take her to parties and dancing venues, and a little-known friend with whom she struck up a friendship and a dating relationship. She occasionally visited a Catholic church looking for spiritual help but did not find it. Despite not being a believer in Christ, she literally felt that God's hand was protecting her, as He delivered her from danger and protected her while she lived alone in that big city.

There we met, and there we fell in love

It was precisely when she returned from New York that we met. She visited her father's agency to visit him, and I saw her there for the first time. At that instant, I didn't have the opportunity to engage her in conversation, and I didn't even know who she was, but I later learned that she was the owner's daughter. About a month later, she returned to the agency to intern at the office before she started studying at the university.

There we met, and there we fell in love. One day someone asked my father-in-law, "Who was I?" My father-in-law replied, "This is someone who wanted to take over my business, but since he couldn't, he took my daughter."

When writing these lines, my father-in-law is 96 years old, strong, and lucid. About four years ago, he received Jesus Christ into his heart. For a long time, we shared the gospel with him, but, as the saying goes, he was a tough nut to crack. Happily, today he has become the most faithful listener of the radio program and does not miss the transmissions of the church services via the internet.

God has given us three wonderful children

God has given us three wonderful children. The oldest, Viviana, after going through a frustrating experience in her marriage, lives alone in Arizona, but maintains daily communication with us and visits us frequently. God has allowed us to see her restoration, little by little, and we can testify to the power of intercessory prayer.

Our second son is Jorge, who has been married to Berny for ten years. They both serve God in the ministry of our church and also work in their respective professions. In addition, they are preparing themselves at LATS and Vanguard University, both Assemblies of God institutions, in order to be prepared for the inevitable call to ministry.

Our third son is Daniel, who also serves God in the ministry of our church while continuing to prepare himself. He also works in one of the most recognized hospitals in Orange County, California.

God brought us to study at Fuller Theological Seminary

God brought the whole family to the United States with the main purpose that I could study at Fuller Theological Seminary in Pasadena, California. It was almost four years of a unique experience, both spiritually and economically, as we left behind our own home, our two vehicles, and good jobs, relying on our savings (which we believed would be sufficient) to face the challenge of growing and being formed in the Word of God.

The savings didn't last even six months; soon, my wife, who already had one job, had to look for another. While in the seminary, I got a job there as a janitor. I had to get up at four in the morning to clean offices, classrooms, and bathrooms and then stay studying for my classes the rest of the day.

Our children never complained

After a few months, my wife got a third job, and I acquired financial help from "World Vision" and quit the janitorial job to dedicate myself fully to my studies. During that time, we lived for a few months on the food given away at the seminary; sometimes, there was chicken, but most days, only canned food. God blessed that food and the people who distributed it. Our children never complained, not even at Christmas, when I told them there would be no gifts, and they accepted it. They put strings of Christmas lights on the wall that formed a tree, and by the grace, mercy, and love of the brethren of the church where we attended, that was the year that our children received the most Christmas gifts.

We began to make plans to return to Guatemala

After completing my studies at Fuller Seminary, we began to make plans to return to Guatemala. Our initial idea was to find a part-time job, either at a university or on my own, and establish a church in our home country. We longed to give ourselves completely to this work. During my time in seminary, I learned about the opportunities that some organizations and denominations offered to start new works by providing financial support to pastors. Despite this, I felt in my heart a desire to continue serving in the Assemblies of God and felt no inclination to join another organization.

However, as we began to make concrete plans to return, we realized that none of our plans were working out. Little by little, God began to confirm that He wanted to use us to minister to Hispanics in the United States, so we accepted the idea of staying in this country.

"The Church in the Home"

By this time, we had started a mission in our home. When we arrived in Pasadena, God had put on our hearts the idea of doing Bible studies and, if possible, starting a ministry in Pasadena by gathering professional people interested in listening to the Word of God. Thus, we gathered some professional couples and invited them to our house on Saturdays; that was how we gathered four couples from different countries and professions. We were able to consolidate one pair that received Jesus Christ. He was a doctor from the Philippines who spoke perfect Spanish and was married to a Salvadoran woman with a law degree. However, despite being thrilled to study the Bible, after two years with us, the other couples did not want to receive the Lord or commit themselves to His work.

So, we opened up the opportunity for all who wanted to join, and along with the professional couple, we opened the mission, which we called, 'The Church in the Home'.

When I finished my studies, and the Lord confirmed that we would stay in California, we began to look for a place to meet and formally establish the mission. Curiously, we knew a family that resided in Costa Mesa, and in spite of the distance, they regularly attended the Sunday meetings of The Church in the Home in

Pasadena. However, not all members of the family were able to join them on each occasion.

Motivated by the desire to provide them with greater closeness and spiritual support, my wife and I made the decision to travel every Friday to Costa Mesa to establish a cell group there. This initiative turned out to be a great blessing, both for the family and for others who joined our meetings.

It was not by accident or mistake!

While looking for a place to establish the church, I received a call from missionary Richard Larson about the possibility of being a candidate for pastor of a church in Costa Mesa. I later learned that my name was given to him by mistake. Actually, he was inquiring about a Guatemalan minister who had been recommended to him, but he had not been given his name. The board member whom he asked, knew me because he had invited me to give a seminar at La Puerta Abierta church in Costa Mesa, and immediately associated him with me and gave my name and phone number to Brother Larson. Of course, we know that it was no accident or mistake, but it was all in God's purpose.

1998: God led us to pastor the Puerta Abierta church in Costa Mesa, CA

That's how, at the end of 1998, God led us to pastor the "La Puerta Abierta" church in Costa Mesa, CA, an established church without a pastor. Most of those who attended 'The Church at Home', came with us to La Puerta Abierta. Only the doctor and his wife, who lived in Pasadena, stayed at another church there.

Eventually, we learned of the trauma, difficulties, and divisions the church had gone through as a growing church. But they had less than 120 members when we became their pastors. We first had to overcome the suspicion, distrust, and prejudice toward the pastors. Now after more than 20 years, we enjoy a special trust and love from the congregation.

The Spirit of the Lord made me understand unequivocally that the church needed a foundation and consolidation in the Word and a permanent and intentional dedication to evangelism. God allowed us to work for three years to consolidate the pastoral ministry and to see the Word of God as essential in the direction of the church. Today our church is a church that loves and respects the Word of God.

God taught me to love

After two years, God gave me a clear vision of how to involve the whole church in reaching the lost. However, before I could carry out this vision, He had to work in my life, teaching me to love all Hispanics and not to make distinctions. I realized that those who would come to our church would not necessarily be the successful professionals I expected, but brokenhearted, oppressed, illegal immigrants, poor, and captives.

Being Guatemalan, God taught me to love my Mexican brothers and sisters, as well as all Central Americans, South Americans, and all those who would become part of the church.

For a whole year, we prepared the church leadership to develop the family group strategy. I had read Dr. Paul Yongi Cho's book on family groups at least fifteen years ago, but after listening to Pastor Edmundo Madrid from Guatemala, God confirmed for me the opportunity to develop my own updated vision of evangelistic family groups to win friends.

The family group strategy

We involved the whole church in this process, starting with the leaders. We announced the changes we were going to implement, and although we had been preparing them for a year, some of them still showed resistance to these changes. Throughout this time, the Lord has given me the opportunity to be invited to many churches to speak about the family group system. Also, many pastors have come to our church seeking to be taught in the development of the evangelistic family group strategy.

However, to this day, I am surprised to see that the great fear of churches and pastors is to change what is already established, even if that system is not working. I do not understand this resistance! The idea is not simply to change for the sake of change, but to find an evangelistic strategy that involves the whole church. It may be another method or approach, but the important thing is to prioritize evangelism since it is the most relevant and urgent thing in our world today. That is why the church was established.

We made the changes because the vision came from God. We involved each and every church member in the family groups. By the way, this is not the Group of Twelve system, it has little or nothing to do with it.

Since we started working with the evangelistic family groups, we have seen excellent results. People started bringing friends and family members to the groups, and then bringing them to church. After two months, we celebrated the first Friend's Day, where seventy-five invited friends came to the church, and fifty of them accepted the Lord Jesus as their Savior. Glory to God!

We immediately established discipleship groups; to disciple and baptize the new converts. Discipleship groups are fundamental because they are like a filter to know who is truly willing to follow Christ. We realized that the parable of the Sower in Matthew 13 contains a great truth; not all who accept the Lord stay. Some seeds fall by the wayside, others in rocky areas or among thorns.

Even so, the church began to grow and develop through evangelistic family groups, and people were motivated and committed. In a couple of years, the church building we were renting, which had a capacity for three hundred people, became too small. We decided to have two services, and soon we had about six hundred people. Even so, a rented place was insufficient because of the inconvenience we had.

In 2005 we rented a church building in Irvine

In 2005, we rented a church building located in Irvine, California, with a capacity of approximately 1,000 people. We were there for about three years and already had about eight hundred members, when we had to move to another location because the building, we were renting was sold, and we had to leave.

Before leaving, God had already given me the vision to look for a place to buy and have our own building. We had already started looking. But the move again to another church in Costa Mesa affected our attendance, mainly because they had dance parties on Saturdays, which affected the testimony of the church. However, we continued to work hard in evangelism through the family groups and in caring for the growing children and youth of the church.

My wife had a calling to work with children

Soon we needed to hire a children's pastor and a youth pastor. Fortunately, in Guatemala, my wife had a calling to work with children and was already in charge of the children's ministry of the church. From then on, the children's ministry began to develop, and to this day, it is one of the pillars of the church. The children's service runs parallel to the adult service, and the children's music and worship groups are the seedbed for the church's adolescent and adult worship groups. The youth groups were growing and consolidating, and we had to develop specific groups for teens and young adults, as they needed a special ministry focus.

While renting in Costa Mesa, the city we had returned to out of necessity, we found an industrial building in Irvine, known as a "warehouse." The building was semi-abandoned and in need of total remodeling.

The economic recession came

We had the promise of financing to buy the building when the economic recession hit the United States (2007-2008), and the bank canceled the loan. After talking to the bank representatives, they recommended that we lease the building with an option to buy, assuring us that once the recession was over, they would grant us a loan. More out of faith than trust in the bank, we decided to take the risk of renting the building, investing in its remodeling, and converting it into a church. At the same time, we continued to pay the rent for the place where we were meeting. It was a bold move, motivated primarily by faith.

In the middle of the recession, we began construction. We had a fund of slightly more than $1,000,000.00, which came from 60% of the tithes collected by the church and 40% from the stewardship campaign we had conducted. This money was earmarked for the down payment on the building and to make the necessary renovations. In the end, we invested a little over $1,500,000 in the remodeling, in addition to the free labor contributed by church members.

In mid-2009, we consulted the bank again to reactivate the loan. After conducting their studies, they informed us that they could not give us the loan due to a 30% decrease in our income.

The God of miracles and a people who live by faith

But God is a God of miracles, and God's people are people who live by faith. After crying out to God, He did the miracle. God provided us with a financier to buy the building and assume the investment in the remodeling as the down payment on the loan.

I have heard pastors say that they did not need a bank loan, that God provided everything, so they did not need a loan. On one occasion, someone asked me, "Don't you have any millionaire members, or anyone with financial solvency who can finance it?" I was speechless. The professionals had stayed in Pasadena, and most of our members were poor immigrants, factory workers, and house cleaners. Yes, they had all been taught to tithe faithfully, and I had witnessed their prosperity.

For us, the miracle had been the loan, and to this day, we have paid it faithfully without any setback. God provided us with a temple large enough for all our activities and a sanctuary for about six hundred people.

143

New churches

God has allowed us to establish two works in California, and to open seven churches in Mexico, all of which are active. At this moment, we are opening a new work in Ensenada, Baja California, and we also have the expectation of opening another one in Mexico City. In addition, we provide support to numerous missionaries around the world. Therefore, church growth cannot be measured solely by attendance at our Irvine church.

When we started the evangelistic family group system, we had eleven groups. Before the pandemic, in 2020, we had managed to expand to about seventy groups. However, as in virtually all churches, we have been affected by the pandemic in terms of attendance and development of the family groups, which has forced us to make drastic adjustments.

Despite this, we have not stopped focusing on evangelism, nor have we stopped prioritizing friendship with those who do not yet know God. We continue to work with the same passion to reach the lost and are willing to make the changes and adjustments necessary for the church to continue fulfilling its mission.

11. BUT THERE'S MORE, SO MUCH MORE

Missionaries Janice & Richard Larson

The last chapter has not been written

In March 2018, my husband Richard and I, with our daughter Cindee and her husband Jason Frenn, were sitting in a large auditorium in Gandía, on the east coast of Spain, awaiting the arrival of the evening's speaker. Jason had participated earlier in the day as a guest speaker.

Meanwhile, my mind wandered back to the years 1978 to 1980, when our family served as missionaries in Spain. Along with missionaries David and Doris Godwin, we planted a church in Madrid, a city of five million people. Although we only had a small part in starting the new church, others did their part, and today, New Life Church, (Nueva Vida) is the largest Assemblies of God church in Madrid.

Now, twenty-five years later, we are seeing how God has blessed the work in Spain. With gratitude in my heart, I thanked God for the privilege of serving Him.

Juan Carlos Escobar, General Superintendent of the Assemblies of God in Spain, went to the platform and preached a message that still impacts us. I remember how he mentioned that in the ancient world, people thought Spain was the end of the world. They believed that if you went through the Strait of Gibraltar and entered the Atlantic Ocean, you would sail to the end of the earth.

Greek mythology tells how Hercules built two pillars or columns near the Strait of Gibraltar to mark the boundary of what was then the known world. These pillars bore the Latin warning, **"Ne Plus ultra"** or **"No Further."** These words warned sailors and navigators that they should go no further; **"There was nothing beyond."**

But Christopher Columbus made his famous voyage and found much more, uniting two worlds. Although the Spanish conquest was a tragic episode and period in the history of Spain and humanity, nevertheless, upon discovering new lands with new opportunities, Spain removed the **"Ne"** from its motto and minted coins with its new motto, **"Plus Ultra,"** meaning **"Beyond."** Thus, breaking that limiting idea that there is nothing more, that this is the best we can aspire to. That this is all there is.

Brother Escobar continued and spoke of the missionaries that Spain has sent, especially to Arab and Muslim countries, because there is a special relationship between Spain and the Moorish people of North Africa. He challenged them not only to reach out to

Spanish-speaking people but to cross cultural barriers to reach people of other origins.

We remember Superintendent Escobar calling the church in Spain to break the mold of believing that they have accomplished all there is, to trust God, believing that He is calling them to do much more. He urged them to be a church that is not content with what they have seen or done in the past, nor with the limitations imposed by others, but to believe that God will help them reach the rest of the world. "Plus Ultra," which means "Beyond." "There is more, much more!"

"Go!" Serving is a Privilege

Dear reader, up to this point, you have read ten stories written by dedicated men and women who, step by step, followed the Lord and became life changers.

Now it's about you and me. God's call is for everyone, not just ministers, pastors or missionaries. We know that deep in the heart exists the desire to be used by God.

Mark 16:15 (NKJV) says, *"And He said to them, "Go into all the world and proclaim the gospel to the whole creation."*

Matthew 28:18-20 (RSV) says, 18 *And Jesus came and said to them, "All authority in heaven and on earth has been given to me. 19 Go therefore and make disciples of all nations, baptizing them in the name of the Father and of the Son and of the Holy Spirit 20 and teaching them to obey everything that I have commanded you. And remember, I am with you always, to the end of the age."[a]*

Jason Frenn: "I consider it an honor and a privilege to be used by the Lord"

Serving God is an exciting and incredible experience. Let me share with you the personal experience of my son-in-law Jason Frenn (with his permission).

Missionary Evangelists Jason and Cindee Frenn held an evangelistic crusade in a marginalized area of San José, the capital of Costa Rica. Thousands of people attended that night.

At the end of the service, people whose lives had been changed and healed, lined up along the altar. As the band began to play, the audience, with hands raised to heaven, began to sing the song, "How Great Thou Art." Suddenly I saw Jason fall to his knees with his face to the ground in worship.

Later I asked him why he had done that. He said, "I was overwhelmed by God's love for these people who are so important to Him. I consider it an honor and a privilege to be used by the Lord to reach out to people."

"Could God use me?" "Would He want to use me?"

As we sit in our comfortable armchairs and read this book, we see that "ordinary" people can do "extraordinary" things when God is involved. Let's ponder the question, "Could God use me? Would He want to use me?"

Every time Rich Guerra, our SoCal Network Superintendent, preaches, he reminds us of a lost world that is waiting to hear the Good News that Jesus died for them.

There are no boundaries or limitations to Jesus' command to GO! Let us destroy the idea that there is nothing more we can accomplish, whether it is across the street or around the world. There is always the possibility of so much more. God will help us to grasp the Dream He has for us. Yes, there is more, much more!

Now back to the question, "Could God use us?" "Does He want to use us?" YES! YES! YES! He wants to use us; He wants to use you and me!

THE LAST CHAPTER HAS NOT YET BEEN WRITTEN!

LET'S WRITE IT!

THE BACK STORY

This book is not about my husband or me, but a little of our story will bring more credibility to the reader.

I am Janice Rood Larson (Juanita), raised in Thief River Falls, Minnesota. My husband, Richard Larson (Ricardo), grew up in Plummer, Minnesota. We are Assemblies of God missionaries.

We first went to Costa Rica in 1966, where we learned to love the latin world. It was in Costa Rica that we adopted our Spanish names: Ricardo y Juanita. We studied Spanish for a year, spent two years ministering to Costa Ricans, and then moved to Panama, the neighboring country to the south, where God called us in the beginning.

Our six years in Panama were years of revival, working and learning from other missionaries, and being part of the founding of the Assemblies of God of Panama. Today, we keep in touch with dozens of ministers and pastors there. If you want more information about our years in Panama, read my book, *"Something Beautiful,"* available on Amazon.

We moved to Spain, where we set up a large yellow and white tent on an empty lot and, together with missionaries David and Doris Godwin, held services every night. Hundreds of people came and accepted Christ as their Savior, and from there, the Nueva Vida (New Life) church of Madrid was born. To learn more, you can read my book, *"Miracles in Madrid,"* available on Amazon.

The SoCal Network (formerly the Southern California District)

The SoCal Network of the Assemblies of God, with a vision to reach their Hispanic neighbors, invited Spanish-speaking

149

missionaries with experience working in Latin America, to come and help them.

Having served in such countries, missionaries Harry and Martha Bartel recognized the need to reach Spanish-speaking people in Southern California. With a passion for souls, they found Hispanics willing to serve and began Sunday School classes or services on weekdays or Sundays, English-speaking churches opened their doors to start a Hispanic ministry. God was moving.

When the Bartels retired, Wayne and Doris Turnbull, missionaries to Mexico, became the first Hispanic Ministries Directors of the SoCal Network. More Hispanic churches and ministries were founded, and gradually Hispanic pastors and leaders came together in a cohesive group. Spanish-language pastors' retreats and camp meetings were initiated at Vanguard University.

Upon the Turnbulls' retirement, it was suggested that Superintendent Ray Rachels contact us to take their place. On January 1998, my husband and I transferred from AGWM (World Missions) to US Missions, moved to Southern California, and were honored to become the new Directors of Hispanic Ministries.

When we arrived, we were welcomed by missionaries Jim and Karla Gutel, who had just been appointed Directors of Intercultural Ministries for the Network. We thank Jim for sharing his small office with my husband and me. Our goal was to be a bridge between the Hispanic churches and the SoCal Network. In 1999, we organized our first Hispanic women's retreat at Pinecrest Christian Center, followed by the Hispanic men's retreat, and continued with Hispanic pastor's retreats. We soon realized the need to have retreats in Spanish for those who were more comfortable in their heart language.

As we became more acquainted with the Hispanic pastors and leaders, we became aware of the importance of extending to them the opportunity for academic preparation for ministry. A Berean Study Center began on March 18, 2005, at the Network Office in Irvine. Classes continued until October 2010, when the Hispanic branch of the School of Ministry (La Escuela de Ministerio) began with us as their directors.

Missionaries Larry and Melodee Gruetzmacher transferred from World Missions to US Missions and served the SoCal Network for several years as Directors of Hispanic Ministries. They greatly expanded the retreats and emphasized church planting.

In 2006 Pablo Kot, Pastor of New Life Assembly in Rosemead, CA, was elected the first Hispanic Presbyter of the SoCal Network. Under his leadership, the Hispanic Fellowship was formed, and Hispanic pastors became leaders in their distinct areas.

These were exciting years. New branches of the Hispanic School of Ministry opened in Santa Maria in 2013 and in Oxnard Evangelistic Center in 2014. The Spanish branch of the School of Ministry's First Graduation was held in the fall of 2014, with twelve students completing the Ordination level. In 2015 my husband and I transferred from the leadership of the Hispanic School of Ministry, and missionary Dan Campbell became the new director. Richard continues on as a professor.

After twenty-five years, many Hispanic pastors now have master's or doctorate degrees and teach most of the classes in the Hispanic School of Ministry (now named Colegio de Ministerio). They are an integral part of the Network, serving in many leadership positions, and their voice is being heard.

Thank God that the younger generation is running strong. God is faithful, and we are very happy to have had a small part in God's plan for the harvest.

Janice (Juanita) Larson   Philippians 4:13

151

Made in the USA
Monee, IL
04 August 2023